Fort Street Methodist Eppiscopal Church,   Ladies Aid Society

Los Angeles Cookery

Fort Street Methodist Eppiscopal Church, Ladies Aid Society

Los Angeles Cookery

ISBN/EAN: 9783744666664

Printed in Europe, USA, Canada, Australia, Japan

Cover: Foto ©Thomas Meinert / pixelio.de

More available books at **www.hansebooks.com**

The Ladies' Aid Society of the Fort street M. E. Church, who are responsible for the publication of this book, desire to express their sincere thanks to the many ladies who have so kindly, cheerfully, and promptly responded in the important matter of furnishing so great a variety of recipes.

In presenting a book comprised entirely of tested recipes, we trust and believe we are furnishing one which will be invaluable to any housekeeper, and especially prized in Los Angeles homes.

LADIES' AID SOCIETY,
Fort street M. E. Church, Los Angeles.

LOS ANGELES, CAL.:
MIRROR PRINTING AND BINDING HOUSE.
1881.

LIST OF CONTRIBUTORS.

Mrs. Anna Ogier,
Mrs. E. F. Spence,
Mrs. Col Geo. Smith,
Mrs. C. G. Du Bois,
Mrs. J. G. Howard,
Mrs. I. W. Hellman,
Mrs. M. E. J.,
Mrs. S B. Caswell,
Miss Mary McLellan,
Mrs. J. G. Eastman,
Mrs. E. S. Chase,
Louise J.
Mrs. M. G. Moore,
Mrs. H. C. Austin,
Miss Rachel Kremer,
Mrs. Theo. Wollweber,
Mrs. Adelia Hall,
Mrs. L. C. Goodwin,
Mrs. Mary Backman,
Mrs. J. R. Toberman,
Mrs. S. C. Foy,
Mrs. E. C. Starin,
Mrs. George Clark,
Mrs. S. Speedy,
Mrs. Dr. Ross,
Mrs. H. K. S. O'Melveny,
Mrs. L. M. Thompson,
Miss M. E. Hoyt,
Mrs. I. R. Dunkelberger,
Reliable,
Mrs. Herbert, Ventura,
Mrs. J. Hines,
Mrs. Barrows,
Mr. E. S. B,
Mrs. J. A. Graves,
Mrs A. A. Dodsworth,
Mrs. Dr French,
Madame Chevalier,
Madame Eugene Meyer,
Mr. J. A. Graves,
Mrs. J. W. Gillette,
Mrs. John Smith,
Mrs. T. S. Stanway,
Mrs E Workman,
Mrs. Mary A. Lindley,
Mrs. I. S. Mayo,

Mrs. J. G. Downey,
Mrs. Henderson,
Mrs. J. E. Hollenbeck,
Mrs. J. M. Stewart,
Mrs. M. M. Templeton,
Miss A. Tuthill,
Mrs. S. H. La Fetra,
Mrs. J. M. Campbell,
Mrs. C. C. Lamb,
Mrs. Dr. Hazeltine,
Mrs. C. H. Bradley,
Mrs. Gen. Stoneman,
Mrs. Jennie Stafford, Santa Ana,
Mrs. Milliken,
Mrs. L. S E. Longstreet,
Mrs. R. N. C. Wilson,
Mrs. F. D. Bovard,
Mrs. Flanders,
Mrs. A. N. Hamilton,
San Gabriel,
Mrs. L. Check.
Mrs. S. Yarnell,
Mrs. John Foy, San Bernardino,
Miss Lillie Milliken,
Mrs. W. W. Widney,
Mrs. Wright, San Bernardino.
Mrs. A. Higbie, Compton,
Mr. L. C. Goodwin,
Mrs. O W. Childs.
Mrs. M. M. Bovard,
Mrs. A. W. Potts,
Mrs. G. Wiley Wells,
Mrs. W. D. Gibbs,
Mrs Chas. Maclay,
Miss A. E Widney,
Mrs. J. C. Newton,
Mrs. H. McLellan,
Miss Mamie Van Doren,
Mrs. John Milner,
Miss Lillie E. Bashford,
Miss Bertha Lindley,
Miss Emma Bradley,
Mrs. H. K. W. Bent,
Mrs. S. C. Hubbell,
Mrs R. M. Widney.

INTRODUCTION.

——:o:——

" Of all appeals—although
I grant the power of pathos and of gold,
Of beauty, flattery, threats, a shilling—no
Methods more sure at moments to take hold
Of the best feelings of mankind, which grow
More tender as we every day behold,
Than that all-softening, over-powering knell,
The tocsin of the soul—the dinner bell."
—*Byron.*

HE present work is not what the Germans call a *versuch*, or what the English call an *essay*, yet it is an *attempt*. Not an attempt to meet a *long felt want*, but to show how, in the best possible way, many *felt* wants may be supplied.

The ladies of the Ladies' Aid Society, of the Fort Street Methodist Episcopal Church, Los Angeles, California, are the authors and publishers of this book. They have two objects in view in sending out the work. First—That of supplying the house-keepers of the country with a large list of tried and valuable recipes. Second—To raise funds to help pay off the indebtedness of the church. Both objects are reasonable and worthy. The recipes are mostly plain and simple, such as every house-keeper will find valuable every day, and are adapted to the poor and rich. Others are for more select dishes, and are more or less expensive. To every recipe is attached the name of the lady furnishing it. Each lady has practically tried those which she furnishes. The book is published for the use of families and is scrupulously temperate. What shall we eat? and how shall it be prepared for our use? are questions which may with propriety exercise the minds of the best scholars and writers in any nation. There are no doubt extremists, epicureans whom the Savior justly rebuked.

The prominence of all bodily appetites and pleasures, and the natural ignorance of, and the not so easily understood character of spiritual pleasures, have led man in his natural condition to exalt, possibly, too much the former. The Esquimaux, according to Dr. Johnson, looks for a heaven where "oil is always fresh and provisions always warm."

The christian, alone, has left out this idea, and given the spiritual heaven. But among the ascetics we find the other extreme. And withal, in the happy medium, there is a true way and a right. Man has a body and it must be cared for as the home of the immortal soul.

The great activities of the soul largely depend on a healthy and well cared for physical being, and may we not say a well-fed physical being. According to Bishop Wiley, a good beefsteak helps to make a good sermon. No doubt but that much of the strong, healthy thought of Old England and the early New England depended on the good, sensible supply of excellent food, which was found always in the larder, and on the table, in the days of yore, in those countries.

The real causes of happiness are *inter præcordia ;* yet human happiness, I dare say, is not wholly independent of good, wholesome living. Cowper says:

> "Now stir the fire and close the shutters fast,
> "Let fall the curtains and wheel the sofa round,
> "And while the bubbling and loud-hissing urn
> "Throws up a steamy column, and the cups
> "That cheer, but not inebriate, wait on each,
> "So let us welcome peaceful evening in."

The formula of Sydney Smith, given to one inquiring how to make home happy, was "always have a bright and cheerful fire, the kettle simmering on the hob, and a paper of sugar plums on the mantle."

A good, wholesome meal is "a great keeper-off of depression" and a great promoter of cheerfulness. I cannot see how any christian can neglect such simple means of happiness and sunshine and then go groaning through this world as a "wilderness of woe," or how they can ask for grace to make them cheerful and happy, and all the while eat unwholesome food, or starve themselves, as a christian duty. God never gives a man grace to make him cheerful with an *empty stomach* when he has supplied him with *daily bread* to satisfy his hunger. The Colony of the Fraternia is a fraud, than which there is none greater except it is the correspondent who lauds and magnifies the Colony. It may be well to state that the people of this Colony live wholly on *raw* fruits and vegetables.

The advance made in producing and preparing articles of food, by the farmer and the merchant, vastly exceeds that made in the kitchen in the art and science of cooking Much of the cooking of to-day is but little in advance of that of a century ago.

And may we not seriously enquire: is not *cooking*, in a certain degree, a lost art? Did not ye house-wives of ye olden time know many ways of serving an excellent dinner, which are wholly unknown to the ladies of the present day? The authors of this book are doing the world a great service in helping on the work of restoration and advance in this most ancient and useful of all arts.

M. M. BOVARD.

———:o:———

GENERAL DIRECTION.—In cooking, as in poetry, architecture and the other fine arts, preserve the unities. A skillful cook may produce a *composition*, such as a mince pie, which the puzzled eater will regard with mingled wonder and delight. But though the cook should not wholly neglect this composite art, for every day comfort cultivate simplicity and directness. Do not let your bread be a puzzle, nor your coffee. If you are asked for a potato, do not cook it in such a manner that the eater will think you did not rightly hear what was asked for. Many eat raw tomatoes or baked potatoes, because that is the only way in which they can get the natural flavor. But a tomato may be cooked so that it will have as distinct and decided a tomato flavor as the raw tomato itself has. So, an apple may be cooked to taste as an apple, a peach to taste as a peach, a turnip as a turnip, and a potato to taste as a potato. Beware of messes. Do not let a stewed chicken remind the eater of boiled pork. Say to your chicken, your coffee, your beefsteak or your potato, as you prepare it for the table, "be yourself, be natural."

E—R.

SOUP DEPARTMENT.

CORN SOUP.

MRS. COL. GEO. SMITH.

Eight tender ears of corn cut or scraped; cook with enough water to boil; boil half an hour, and then add two quarts of new milk; let that boil, and put into it two table-spoons of butter, rubbed into three teaspoons of flour. Let it all boil once more, adding pepper and salt. Beat into the tureen three eggs, stirring briskly while the boiling soup is poured on. This soup should be stirred often while cooking.

———:o:———

GREEN PEA SOUP.

MRS. C. G. DU BOIS.

Boil three pints of green peas in just enough water to boil them; then pour in three pints of milk, and when it boils stir in one-fourth pound of butter, in which a table-spoon of flour has been mixed; stir it until it boils; season with salt and pepper.

———:o:———

AMBER SOUP.

MRS. J. G. HOWARD.

Take a shin of beef, and about a pound of the meat cut up small; put three or four slices of salt pork into a pan and fry them crisp; take out the pork, slice three or four small onions, put into the fat and brown carefully; take the onions out, put in the reserved meat and fry brown and crisp; put the pork, meat and onions with the rest of the meat and bone into the soup kettle; add as in beef soup a couple of carrots, a turnip, some celery and a few bay leaves; pack down, cover with water and heat gradually; boil slowly six hours; strain and set away. Next day skim and strain through a coarse cloth into the soup kettle; stir in the whites and broken shells of two eggs to clear it, and as the scum boils up take it off; season with salt and pepper and a little mace. A few peeled slices of lemon may be added.

————:o:————

OYSTER SOUP.

MRS. C. G. DU BOIS.

To one quart of oysters one quart of water; boil up with liquor and skim; four eggs well beaten with one pint of milk; one large spoon of butter rubbed in flour; salt and pepper.

————:o:————

TOMATO SOUP.

MRS. S. B. CASWELL.

One can of tomatoes (or one quart of ripe tomatoes), to one quart of milk; boil the tomatoes at least half an hour, then strain and let it cool; put it with the cold milk a spoonful first at a time; season with salt, pepper and butter. Put it on the stove and stir until it is thoroughly heated—*not boiled.*

————:o:————

GUMBO SOUP.

MRS. ANNA OGIER.

Boil a shin of beef an hour; pour off the water; let it boil an hour longer, then put in salt to taste. This will make two and one-half gallons of gumbo; when you add to it a half gallon of sliced okra, the same of peeled tomatoes, four large onions, three pods of green peppers; let all boil together for five hours, slowly, so as not to scorch; then add a half-pint of rice, nicely boiled, and let it cook half an hour longer. This is the very best and most nutritious soup ever made, and a great Southern dish.

————:o:————

GERMAN GUMBO SOUP.

MRS. I. W. HELLMAN.

Take a young chicken or the half of a full grown one, mix together flour, pepper and salt; roll the fowl in it and then drop it in hot lard and fry nice and brown. Cut okra up in rounds until there is over a quart of cut okra; when the chicken is nearly done add this to it, and fry about ten minutes, stirring all of the time; do not allow this to brown. Next pour on two quarts of boiling water, and drop in a slice of ham; boil this down to one and one-half quarts. If you desire, about ten minutes before taking it off the fire, add two dozen *fresh* oysters and their juice. There must be rice cooked to eat with Gumbo, and it must be perfectly done and dry. When serving the soup place a large spoonful of rice in each plate and pour the gumbo over it.

————:o:————

BROWN FLOUR SOUP.

MRS. M. E. J.

Take common stock; brown a teacup of flour; add to the soup until sufficiently thickened. Stir in, just before the soup is served, a tablespoonful of cloves and allspice. Salt and pepper to taste.

————:o:————

CHICKEN AND OYSTER SOUP.

MRS. A. HIGBIE, COMPTON.

One full-grown chicken; just enough water to cover it; simmer it gently; when done, take the chicken out, strain the liquor; add one quart of sweet milk to one of broth, if not enough broth add sufficient boiling water; then one quart of oysters with their juice; a blade of mace; one table-spoon of butter; one of arrow-root; flour rubbed into the butter; one gill of hot cream; stew gently five minutes; use the chicken for salad. Cream should always be boiled before being put into soup or gravy.

————:o:————

BEEF SOUP.

MISS MARY MCLELLAN.

Three pints of beef stock; half an onion and one small potato finely chopped. Boil one hour. Add one and one-half cups of stewed tomatoes; salt and pepper; boil half an hour and strain. Add two well-beaten eggs, mixed with a little cold soup (to prevent the eggs curdling), and serve.

————:o:————

MILK SOUP.

ANONYMOUS.

Four large potatoes; two leeks; two ounces of butter; three tablespoonfuls of crushed tapioca; one pint of milk. Put the potatoes and leeks, cut in four, in a sauce pan, with two quarts of boiling water; two ounces of butter; a tea-spoonful of salt, and pepper to taste; boil one hour; rub through a colander, and return to the saucepan; add the milk; sprinkle in the tapioca, and let it boil fifteen minutes.

———— :o:————

TOMATO SOUP.

MISS MARY MCLELLAN.

One quart can of tomatoes; if not well dissolved, chop them fine and boil ten minutes; add one-fourth teaspoonful of soda and stir till it ceases to effervesce. Then add two Boston crackers, pounded fine; season with butter, salt and pepper; add one quart of milk and boil ten minutes.

FISH DEPARTMENT.

SCALLOPED OYSTERS.

MRS. J. G. EASTMAN.

One quart of oysters; one cupful dry bread-crumbs; two spoonfuls butter; one-half cup of cream; pepper and salt to taste. Cover the bottom of a buttered baking-dish with crumbs; wet these with the cream; pepper and salt, and strew with small pieces of butter; then put in the oysters, with a little of their liquor; pepper them, strew pieces of butter over them, and cover with dry crumbs; put more butter on top. Set in the oven, and bake until the juice bubbles up to the top; then set the dish for a few moments on the upper grating of the oven to brown. Send to table in the baking-dish.

————:o:————

SCALLOPED OYSTERS.

MRS. E. S. CHASE.

Do not drain the liquor from the oysters, but fish them out of it as you use them; in that way as much liquor as you require adheres to them; use stale bread, and do not crumble too fine, or it will be clammy; half a teaspoonful of cream, two great teaspoonfuls of butter, salt and pepper; oysters part with a great deal of moisture in cooking, and if the mixture is too wet it is not good; it should be rather dry when done. Cover the bottom of a well-buttered baking-dish with a layer of very dry bread crumbs; dust over a litte salt and pepper, and stick little bits of butter all over the crumbs; then, with a spoon, moisten it with the cream; next place a layer of oysters, alternating with bread crumbs, until the dish is filled, finishing with the butter and cream; invert a plate over it to keep in the flavor. Bake three-fourths of an hour, or until the juice bubbles up to the top; remove the plate, and brown on the upper shelf of the oven for two or three minutes only.

————:o:————

FISH BALLS.

MRS. HAZELTINE.

Take the fish left from dinner; put in your chopping tray, being careful there are no bones in it; chop fine; pare or boil potatoes enough to have twice the quantity of potatoes that you have of fish. When cooked, turn them into the tray with the fish; mash fine, and to a quantity that will make a dozen balls; add one egg, butter the size of an egg, salt and pepper; shape and fry in butter or lard.

————:o:————

FISH CHOWDER.

MRS. E. S. CHASE.

Cut the fish into small pieces; put a layer of fish in the bottom of the kettle, in which sprinkle salt and pepper; next a layer of sliced potato, then another layer of fish (sprinkle well with pepper and salt), until you have the desired quantity; put in cold water enough to cover; let cook until the potato is done (15 to 20 minutes); add one cup of milk, a piece of butter half the size of an egg, flour enough to thicken. Serve in soup dishes.

————:o:————

BAKED WHITE FISH.

MRS. J. G. EASTMAN.

Clean the fish, but do not cut off the head and tail; stuff it with a dressing made of half a pound of bread-crumbs, soaked in water till soft, and then pressed free from the water; mix with the crumbs two tablespoonfuls of minced onion, some butter, chopped parsley, pepper and salt, and a beaten egg. When the fish is stuffed, wrap a piece of cord around it to keep the dressing in. Put slices of salt pork on the top of the fish, sprinkle it with pepper and salt, put some hot water in the pan, and bake in a hot oven, basting frequently. When done, it should be a fine brown. If the fish is large, it will take an hour to bake it. When done, take it up and boil up the gravy with a tablespoonful of catsup, a tablespoonful of flour, wet with cold water and the juice of a lemon; pour this sauce over the fish, and serve. Any fish may be baked in this way.

————:o:————

BAKED FISH.

LOUISEJ.

Take the upper half of the fish, clean and wipe it very dry; make a dressing of bread-crumbs and chopped fat pork; season with salt, pepper, thyme and marjoram; fill the belly of the fish; secure it well, then lay it on a pan, with slices of pork over it, and a little water, and bake one or one and a half hours, according to the size of the fish. Drawn butter for baked or boiled fish; put into one pint of boiling water one-half pound butter, and one teaspoonful of corn-starch, mixed with a little water; boil ten minutes. Serve in a gravy tureen, with either chopped parsley or two hard-boiled eggs, chopped fine.

————:o:————

CODFISH BALLS.

MRS. J. G. EASTMAN.

Cut the codfish in pieces, taking out the bones and skin; then shred it and put it on the stove in some cold water. As soon as it begins to boil change the water. Repeat this process until the fish is tender and free from salt. Do not let it boil or it will be tough. When it is done mix it with twice the quantity of mashed potatoes. Form them into cakes, adding to the mixture a little butter and a beaten egg; flour the cakes and fry them a light brown in boiling lard.

————:o:————

A GOOD WAY TO COOK FISH.

MRS. M. G. MOORE.

If in the brine, soak well, then lay them in a dripping pan and cover well with good, thick, sweet cream. You can add pepper to the cream, if you wish, also a small piece of butter. Now place the dripping pan in the oven and cook till thoroughly done. If the fish are fresh, salt before cooking.

————:o:————

CLAM FRITTERS.

MRS. J. G. EASTMAN.

Stew the clams until done; then take them off the stove; remove the hard edge; chop them into mincemeat and pour them into a batter made of one cup of milk, two cups flour, four eggs, a little salt and a teaspoonful yeast powder. Mix the clams thoroughly into this batter and fry in hot lard.

————:o:————

FRIED FISH OF ANY KIND.

MRS. H. C. AUSTIN.

Clean, wash and dry the fish; lay them in a large flat dish; salt and dredge with flour. If the fish are large and thick, slice them; have ready a frying pan of hot lard or butter; put them in and fry to a good brown.

————:o:————

POTTED TROUT.

MRS. M. G. MOORE.

Take one dozen trout; dress and wipe with a dry cloth; strew a little salt in and over them, and let them lie all night; then wipe them again, with a dry cloth and season with one ounce of white pepper, one-fourth ounce of cayenne, one-half ounce pounded cloves and a pinch of mace. Clarify two pounds of butter; then put the fish, with their backs down, in a pot lined with paper; pour the butter over them, and bake for four hours in a slow oven.

------:o:------

FRIED TROUT.

MRS. J. G. EASTMAN.

Clean, wash and dry the fish; salt and pepper them; roll lightly in flour or corn meal, and fry quickly in boiling lard. Take them up as soon as done and lay upon a hot, folded napkin to absorb the grease; then place them side by side in a heated dish and send to the table.

------:o:------

FISH CHOWDER.

MRS. H. C. AUSTIN.

Take a pound of salt pork, cut into strips and soak for five minutes; cover the bottom of the pot with a layer of this; cut four pounds of cod or sea-bass into pieces two inches square, and lay enough of this over the pork to cover it; then chopped onions, (these may be omitted if desired); parsley, summer savory, and pepper, also crackers. Repeat this layering until your fish and pork are used. Cover with cold water and boil gently for an hour. Then take out the thick part with a skimmer, and after thickening the other with a little flour and butter, pour it over that you have skimmed out.

------:o:------

FISH CHOWDER.

MRS. J. G. EASTMAN.

Take a pound of salt pork; cut it into strips and fry. Cover the bottom of a pot with a layer of this; cut four pounds of cod, or any other large fish, into small pieces and put a layer of this on the pork; then a layer of onion, sliced thin, with salt and pepper; next a layer of crackers, moistened with hot water; then the pork again, the fish, onion, seasoning and cracker. The top layer must be buttered cracker. Cover the whole with cold water. Stew gently for an hour, keeping it covered with water. When it is done thicken with a tablespoonful of flour and the same quantity of butter.

——:o:——

BAKED FISH.

LOUISEJ.

Clean and stuff with dressing made of slices of bread well buttered; a small onion chopped fine; salt and pepper, and soften with hot water; then sew it up; lay it on skewers in the baking pan, with a cupful of water; baste it often with butter and water, and bake one hour until tender and brown. Take it up and put on hot dish, and take out threads, and garnish with sliced lemon and parsley; thicken gravy with a little flour and butter and lemon juice, and serve in a sauce boat.

Louisej is thoroughly reliable.—EDS.

——:o:——

CLAM CHOWDER.

MRS. R. M. WIDNEY.

Take six tablespoonfuls of pickled pork cut into dice; two medium-sized onions and one desertspoon of butter, and fry thoroughly; then add two tablespoons of flour; bronw well and place on the back of the stove. Put one quart of clams over the fire in their own liquor; when they have boiled three minutes, strain them and return the liquor to the fire; add to the liquor the fried pork and onions; one quart of milk; one pint of cream; one quart of potatoes, cut in dice, and salt to taste. When about to send to table, add the clams chopped fine, one and one half pints of toasted bread, cut in dice, and a little thyme.

——-:o:———

TO COOK CODFISH.

MRS. C. G. DUBOIS.

Shred about two-thirds of a quart of codfish; wash it with fresh cool water, and let it soak in cold water until quite fresh; drain off the water and put it in a saucepan with a pint of sweet cream and one-half pint of sweet milk; let it come to a boil; beat together one egg and tablespoonful of flour, and two tablespoonfuls of milk; put into saucepan and stir continually till done; add butter, the size of a butternut; serve on buttered toast.

———:o:———

BAKED SHAD.

MRS. M. E. J.

Clean and stuff with force meat; lay at length in the pan; pour in one pint of water and a gill of mushroom catsup; add pepper, a little vinegar, salt, six cloves and two cloves of garlic; baste well while baking; when done remove to the platter, and stir the gravy till sufficiently reduced; thicken with butter and browned flour, and pour over the fish.

———:o:———

SAUCE HOLLANDAISE.

MISS RACHEL KREMER.

To be used with boiled fish.—Take a large piece of unsalted butter, put it in a ban marie (a sort of double saucepan, used generally for boiling milk); when melted, pour it on the yolks of two or three uncooked eggs, stirring slowly all the time; add a little of the water the fish has been boiled in, a little salt, and some lemon juice. Sauce: The yolks of two hard-boiled eggs, with a teaspoonful of English mustard, a teaspoonful of anchovy butter, the green of an onion, well mashed, or chives, if you can get them, oil and vinegar. Mix these ingredients as in mayonaise.

————:o:————

BOILED MACKEREL.

MRS. M. E. J.

When the fish has been cooked until tender in boiling water, remove the back-bone and sprinkle the inner surface with chopped parsley; brown butter the size of an egg; add a dash of vinegar; mix well and pour over the opened fish; clap together and serve.

————:o:————

HERRING.

MRS. THEO. WOLLWEBBER.

Take the herring, and clean very nicely; soak in milk over night. When ready for use put them on a platter, cover with onions, cut very fine; take the milt, a spoonful of vinegar, one of sweet oil; keep adding oil and vinegar until the milt is dissolved, then pour through a wire sieve over the fish.

————:o:————

TO STEW FISH WITH EGGS AND LEMONS.

MISS RACHEL KREMER.

For this stew, some firm white fish is the best. After the fish is cleaned, slice about an inch and a half in thickness; season with salt, pepper and ginger, then set it aside. Soak about half a loaf of bread in water; when well soaked, squeeze dry, then take some stale bread and grate it; mix this with the soaked bread; chop a small slice of the fish very fine, also parsley and two eggs, and add to the bread; season with ginger, pepper and salt to taste; make small balls of this mixture, which are to be cooked with the fish. Now take two teaspoons of olive oil, in a stew-pan, with some chopped up onion, fry to a light brown, and add a cup of water and a half cup of vinegar. Then put fish in kettle, next balls, taking care not to allow them to break; if there is not sufficient water and vinegar to cover the fish well, add more, always having half as much vinegar as water; allow it to cook slowly until quite done. While it is cooking, squeeze two large lemons, being careful that the seeds do not mix with the juice. Separate the whites from the yolks of two or three eggs, and pour the lemon juice slowly into the yolks. When the fish is thoroughly cooked, pour the hot juice very slowly and carefully into the eggs and lemon, taking great care that it does not curdle. (You need not make use of all the hot juice, add as much as you wish, for this is only a sauce.) Pour sauce over fish again, and set on back of stove until it thickens, not allowing it to come to a boil. Dish slowly and carefully, so that every piece, also the balls, come out whole. Garnish the dish with parsley. This preparation is to be eaten cold.

————:o:————

CRAB CREOLE.

MRS. M. E. J.

Take three large crabs or lobsters; pick fine, after they have been boiled; place in a deep baking dish; alternate layers of crab seasoned with made mustard, cayenne, salt, butter and chopped parsley, and layers of bread crumbs till the dish is filled; then pour milk over it till it will absorb no more; let the top layer be bread crumbs with little dabs of butter strewn over; bake until brown.

MEAT DEPARTMENT.

BROILING.

MRS. ADELIA HALL.

This is not only the most rapid manner of cooking meat, but is justly a favored one. It has nearly the same effect upon meat as roasting; the albumen of the outer portions is hardened, and, forming a skin, retains the juices. It should be turned rapidly in order to produce an equal effect, but the meat should not be punctured with a fork. Salt meat should be put into cold water, and boil slowly. A red pepper dropped in the water will prevent the rising of an unpleasant odor. Fresh meat, unless for soup, should be put into boiling water and allowed to cook very gently; no salt to be added until nearly done. In roasting, put into a hot oven, and baste frequently.

————:o:————

BROILED STEAK.

MRS. L. C. GOODWIN.

Have the gridiron smoking hot; place the platter designed for the steak in the oven to heat; put the steak on the hot iron; for a medium sized steak it will not be necessary to turn more than once; when done remove to the platter, and add butter, pepper and salt; put in the oven for a few moments, and send hot to the table.

————:o:————

POTTED BEEF.

MRS. MARY BACKMAN.

Beef flank 10 pounds; take off the outside skin, salt and pepper thoroughly, then roll and tie; put in a flat pot, with three pints of water, add tablespoonful each of whole cloves and of allspice; boil two hours; take off cover and roast down; keep turning; roast to a light brown.

———:o:———

SPANISH HASH.

MRS. J. R. TOBERMAN.

Chopped meat, one pint; chopped onions, one cup; three tomatoes, chopped fine. Roast five large red chillies in a hot oven; when a light brown throw them into a little hot water; rub thoroughly till the pulp separates from the skins; pass the pulp through a cullender. Put a little lard in a frying pan; add the onions and tomatoes and fry a light brown; add the chopped meat and red pepper sauce, and a little salt; stew fifteen minutes.

———:o:———

TO CORN BEEF.

MRS. S. C. FOY.

Take twelve or fifteen pounds of beef, cut from the round; cut it into four pieces; put it into a jar or cask; cover it with brine made as follows: To one gallon boiling water dissolve rock salt until, when cold, a fresh egg will float; one teaspoonful of saltpetre will give the meat a red color; turn a plate over the meat, and weight it down with a stone. In about four days pour off the brine, boil it, skim it, cool it, and pour it over the meat again. Six days will corn thoroughly.

———:o:———

STUFFED CHILLIES.

MRS. J. R. TOBERMAN.

Take twelve large green bell chillies; roast them on bright coals, and put them in hot water to remove the skins; cut off the stem ends, remove the seed and veins, and fill with the following dressing: Take cold beef, pork or veal, chopped fine; add chopped onions, with bread crumbs, and season with butter, salt and pepper to taste; bake in a quick oven fifteen minutes; serve hot with roast beef, or as a side dish.

———:o:———

HAM TOAST.

MRS. S. C. HUBBELL.

One quarter of a pound of lean ham chopped fine; beat well the yolks of three eggs; one tablespoonful of melted butter; two tablespoons of cream, or good milk; stir over the fire till it thickens, and spread on hot toast.

———:o:———

MOCK DUCK.

MRS. E. C. STARIN.

Take a flank steak; make a dressing the same as for ducks; spread it on the steak; then roll up and tie tight with a string to keep it in shape; lay in a platter with a little water; sprinkle with pepper and salt, and bake.

———:o:———

HASH CAKES.

MRS. MARY BACKMAN.

Two pounds of cold roast or corned beef, six large potatoes, one raw onion; chop fine; salt and pepper to taste; make in balls; roll into flour, then fry in hot lard.

———:o:———

SPICED BEEF.

MRS. GEORGE CLARK.

Procure from eight to ten pounds of ribs of beef—those with considerable fat on are best; remove the bone, rub the meat well with one ounce of salt-petre, pounded fine.   Three hours after this has been applied, rub on a half-pound of moist sugar; let the meat lie in this for two days. Take one ounce of ground pepper, one ounce of pounded mace, a few cloves, likewise well pounded, and a teaspoonful of cayenne pepper; mix all together thoroughly, and rub well into the beef, particularly into the holes, adding occasionally a little salt. Roll up the meat as a round, and bind it with a strong fillet. Chop some shredded suet fine, and cover the beef with it. Put a cupful of water in the baking-pan, and bake in a moderately heated oven from five to six hours.

————:o:————

MEAT BALLS.

MRS. J. R. TOBERMAN.

Chop one teacupful of ham; mix with a pint of mashed potatoes, and one or two well-beaten eggs; a little salt and pepper, and a wee bit of mustard, sage, or sweet marjoram; roll in balls and fry in hot lard.

————:o:————

SLICED MUTTON WITH MUSHROOMS.

MRS. M. E. J.

Cut meat thin, no fat or skin; flour both sides; take six large mushrooms, cut up in four pieces, put in to stew with a piece of butter; add a little stock, pepper and salt. When done, put in the meat; heat slowly; stir frequently; don't boil it. As soon as done, and the gravy thickens, serve on toast, or fried bread around the dish.

————:o:————

BEEF A' LA MODE.

MRS. S. SPEEDY.

A round of beef, cut out the bone, and fill the place with a rich stuffing of bread-crumbs, onions, a lump of butter the size of an egg, one egg. Have ready one teaspoonful of salt, pepper, cloves and mace, mix all together; make incisions in the beef with a knife, and put in strips of fat pork rolled in the spices; sprinkle the remainder of the spices over the beef, then cover the whole with fat pork to prevent its burning. Tie the beef around to keep it in place; place in an oven, with three quarts of water; bake five hours; baste it often with lard and butter mixed in flour. When done, skim off the fat and thicken the gravy; season with walnut, catsup and mace.

————:o:————

HAM SANDWICHES.

MRS. DR. ROSS.

Five pounds of cold boiled ham and two fresh beef-tongues. Chop together, *very fine;* then add one teaspoonful dry mustard, one tablespoonful white sugar, one teaspoonful pepper. Moisten the meat by stirring into it two well-beaten eggs. Spread between thin slices of buttered bread. This quantity will make a hundred sandwiches.

————:o:————

SAUSAGE STEW.

MRS. H. K. S. O'MELVENY.

Make a thick layer of slices of peeled potatoes, sprinkle on a little salt, and then cut up sausages over the potatoes. Continue alternate layers of potatoes and sausages—the top layer being potatoes—pour in a little water, and stew.

————:o:————

STEAK WITH ONIONS.

MRS. ANNA OGIER.

Take a porterhouse steak; have the frying pan very hot and grease with hot lard, so the steak will crisp quickly. After it has crisped on both sides, remove to dish and keep on stove. Have two large onions chopped and scalded with boiling water; then put them into the pan from which the steak has been removed; salt and pepper and fry to a light brown; then add a spoon of butter, dredge with flour; add as much milk or cream as will make a nice gravy. Let it come to a boil and pour over the steak.

————:o:————

VEAL LOAF.

MRS. L. M. THOMPSON.

Take three pounds of raw veal and one pound of salt pork, ten large crackers, one teaspoonful of pepper, and one of sage; chop well together, season with salt, and add three eggs and a half-teacup of cream. Make into a loaf, and bake three hours; baste often with butter and water.

————:o:————

PATE DE VEAU.

M. E. HOYT.

Three and one-half pounds of leg of veal, fat and lean; six small crackers; one slice of fat pork; two eggs; one tablespoonful of black pepper; one nutmeg. Chop all the ingredients very fine and mix them; beat the eggs and add them to the mixture, together with a piece of butter the size of an egg, and a tablespoonful of salt; roll in a ball and bake in a pan or dish for an hour and a half.

———— — :o:————

SPICED BEEF.

MRS. I. R. DUNKELBERGER.

Take the brisket; cut it into pieces the size you wish to cook; rub them with fine salt, a little sugar, cloves, allspice, pepper and saltpetre; roll the beef up tight and tie it; to thirty pounds of beef allow a cup of salt, a cup of spice (whole), a piece of saltpetre the size of a nutmeg, broken fine; when prepared pack into a keg; add one quart of white wine vinegar, and enough brine to cover the beef. In one week it

will be fit for use and will keep six months.   A piece weigh-
ing eight pounds must be boiled six hours; press eight hours;
serve cold with any sauce preferred.   Worcestershire is usually given the preference.

————:o:————

BEEF A LA MODE.

MRS. H. K. S. O'MELVENY.

Take a round of beef; make incisions all through it;
then roll strips of raw salt pork, in a seasoning made of
thyme, cloves, pepper and salt, half a teaspoonful of each,
and draw them through the holes made in the beef; put in
a pot with some small onions and a quarter of pound of butter; pour on enough hot water to cover it and cook slowly
three or four hours.

————:o:————

POTTED MEAT.

MRS. M. G. MOORE.

Cut the meat from the bone; chop fine and season
highly with pepper and salt, cloves and cinnamon; moisten
with vinegar, Worcester sauce or butter melted, according
to the kind of meat used or to suit your taste.   Pack it tight
in a stone jar and cover the top with about one-forth inch of
melted butter.   It will keep for months and always affords an
excellent dish for tea.

————:o:————

TO MAKE BRAWN—ENGLISH.

ANONYMOUS.

Two hours and a half or three hours.   A pig's head of
six or seven pounds, one and three-quarter pounds of lean
beef, four or five cloves, pepper, salt and cayenne pepper.
Clean the pig's head thoroughly, put into a stew-pan with
about a pound and three quarters of lean beef, cover with
cold water, and boil until the bones can be removed, skim-

ming frequently. Put the meat into a hot pan before the fire, and mince it as fine as possible, and as quickly; season well with the spices, pepper, salt and cayenne; stir briskly together, and press in a brawn-tin or cake mould with a very heavy weight, until quite cold and thoroughly set. When required for use, dip the mould into boiling water, and turn the brawn out on a dish.

————:o:————

LIVER CHEESE.

MRS. HERBERT, VENTURA.

Boil a beef's liver, heart and tongue; remove all the hard sinewy parts, and chop the remainder fine; add to this, half pound of salt pork, also chopped fine; season it all well, put into a pan and press it hard. After standing a few hours it will come out in a solid cake, and is very nice to slice for breakfast or lunch.

————:o:————

ROAST BEEF—GERMAN.

MRS. THEO. WOLLWEBER.

If your roast is secured the night before using, roll it in a cloth wet with vinegar; if not, take a piece of the round, not too large, a piece of butter, one or two onions sliced, two carrots, two or three tomatoes, salt and pepper. Put in a kettle, cover closely and steam until done and brown, adding vinegar or water to taste, and basting frequently. When almost finished thicken with bread crumbs. Strain the sauce before sending to table.

————:o:————

WARMED-OVER MEATS.

MRS. M. G. MOORE.

A good way to use cold bits of fish—Pick the fish from the bones into small pieces; cut two or three small potatoes up pretty fine; melt some butter in the spider; add a little cream, then put fish and potatoes into this, and pepper and salt. Stir frequently till heated through, not browned; just before lifting to the dish add one or two well-beaten eggs. Serve hot. Nice for breakfast.

———:o:———

ANOTHER.

MRS. M. G. MOORE.

Cut slices of cold roasted meat and mince it very fine; brown some flour in butter, and moisten with stock or water; add salt and pepper and let it simmer ten minutes; add some more butter and some gherkins cut in slices; then add the minced meat and let simmer slowly, not boil. Use parsley and capers with mutton instead of gherkins.

———:o:———

VEAL POT-PIE.

MRS. J. HINES.

Cut the meat into small pieces; place in a pot and cook with little water; when cooked, thicken the gravy and season to taste. Make a light crust and cut up in square pieces; drop into the kettle and cover up tight.

———:o:———

TO BAKE A HAM.

MRS. S. SPEEDY.

Take a nice plump ham, scrape and wash nicely. Have ready a dough made of flour and water; roll out about an inch thick, and cover your ham completely with this, wetting the edges to prevent exposing the ham. Bake three hours.

———:o:———

BREAKFAST FRITTERS.

MRS. DR. ROSS.

Chop very fine any kind of cold meat—though veal or ham is the nicer. For one cup of minced meat take one cup of sweet milk, one egg, tablespoonful bread-crumbs, and one of flour; add a little pepper and salt, and fry to a light brown, as you would small butter-cakes.

————:o:————

A NICE WAY OF COOKING COLD MEATS.

MRS. BARROWS.

Chop the meat fine, season with salt, pepper and a little onion, or else tomato catsup; fill a bread-pan two-thirds full, cover it over with mashed potato, which has been salted, and has milk in it; lay bits of butter over the top, and set it into the oven for fifteen or twenty minutes.

————:o:————

OMELET OF VEAL.

MRS. C. G. DU BOIS.

Take two pounds of veal, chopped fine, eight grated crackers, one spoon sage, same of pepper and salt, four eggs, one teacup of sweet milk, one-half butter; mix all well together, and bake one and a half hours.

————:o:————

SCRAPPLES.

MRS. HERBERT, VENTURA.

Take a pig's head, boil it until the meat cleaves from the bone; cut it fine, mix it in the liquor it was boiled in, with Indian meal, pepper, salt and herbs to suit the taste. Boil until it is about the consistency of mush. Let it cook, cut in slices, fry in lard. It will keep two or three weeks.

————:o:————

HUNTER'S ROAST.

MRS. R. M. WIDNEY.

Ingredients—One leg mutton; one pound smoked bacon. Preparation—Cut the bacon in slices about two inches long and three-fourths inch; make insertions or pockets near the surface of the mutton and insert the bacon. Roast in usual manner. The slips of bacon should be so inserted that the fat from the bacon, while roasting will drain down through the mutton to flavor it.

— — —:o:— — —

SPICED VEAL.

MRS. C. G. DU BOIS.

Take some of the thick loin of veal; cut it into small pieces, and pour over it as much hot spiced vinegar as will cool it. To one-half pint of vinegar put a teaspoonful of allspice, a very little mace, salt and cayenne pepper.

— — —:o:— — —

HAMBERGER STEAK.

MRS. J. A. GRAVES.

Equal parts of beef, veal and pork, chopped fine; season with pepper, salt, thyme and nutmeg, grated lemon peel and the juice of one lemon, eggs and bread crumbs; shape into oblong form and cover thickly with flour; bake and baste often.

— — —:o:— — —

TO CURE 1,000 HAMS.

MR. E. S. B.

Sixty pounds of salt; three gallons of molasses; two and one-half pounds of potash; one-quarter pound of saltpetre. Pack and fill up with well or spring water; lie in brine five weeks and then they are ready to smoke.

— — —:o:— — —

BEEF–STEAK PIE.

MRS. BARROWS.

Take cold roast beef, cut it into thin slices, about an inch long; take raw potatoes, peel them, and cut them in thin slices. Have ready a deep dish; lay some of the potatoes on the bottom, then a layer of beef, and so on until the dish is filled; season it as you would chicken pie; fill it with boiling water, cover with a crust, and bake it.

———:o:———

BOILED TONGUE.

MRS. ADELIA HALL.

In choosing a tongue ascertain how long it has been dried or pickled, and select one with a smooth skin, which denotes its being young and tender; if a dried one, and rather hard, soak it at least for twelve hours before cooking it; if, however, it is fresh from the pickle, two or three hours will be sufficient for it to remain in soak; put the tongue in a stew-pan, with plenty of cold water and a bunch of savory herbs; let it gradually come to a boil; skim well and simmer gently until tender; peel off the skin, garnish with tufts of celery or parsley sprouts, and serve. Boiled tongue is frequently sent to table with boiled poultry instead of ham, and is, by many, preferred; if served cold, peel it; fasten it down to a piece of board by sticking a fork through the root and another through the top, to straighten it; garnish with parsley. A large tongue needs to be cooked between four and five hours, a small one, between two and three hours.

———:o:———

BRAINS.

MRS. M. E. J.

Scald, clean and stew in one-quarter pound of butter, a tablespoonful of fine parsley, juice of a lemon, and salt and pepper.

———:o:———

BRAINS BAKED.

MRS. M. E. J.

Clean and stew until done; mix with one egg; season as before, except parsley: add a tablespoonful of butter;

mix with fine bread crumbs, and heap in a tin plate. Strew the top with crumbs and pieces of butter; brown in the oven.

————:o:————

TONGUE CHEESE.

MRS. A. A. DODSWORTH.

One beef's tongue, two calves' livers, three pounds salt pork; boil until well done; mince very fine; season to taste (with spice, if desired); press in a pan or mold until cold, then it is ready to slice and serve. Makes a delicious cold dish for lunch.

————:o:————

BROILED TRIPE.

ANONYMOUS.

Prepare tripe as for frying; lay it on a broiling iron, over a clear fire; let it broil gently; when one side is done turn the other side; take it up on a hot dish, butter it; garnish with lemon or parsley.

————:o:————

FRIED TRIPE.

MRS. DR. FRENCH.

Having boiled the tripe until perfectly tender all through, cut into pieces three or four inches square; make a batter of four eggs, four tablespoons flour, and a pint of milk; season with nutmeg; dip each piece of tripe twice into the batter, then fry it in hot butter or lard.

————:o:————

BRAINS.

MRS. ANNA OGIER.

Parboil them, let them cool, and skin them; careful not to break; cut in slices about an inch wide; dredge with corn meal, pepper and salt; fry in hot lard; garnish with double-leaf parsley.

————:o:————

TO FRY TRIPE.

ANONYMOUS.

Take prepared tripe, wash and wipe dry; cut it four inches square; dip first in egg, then flour; let it fry gently to a delicate brown, in butter, if liked; add to the gravy a wine glass of vinegar and water; boil up, and pour over the dish with the tripe.

————:o:————

HEAD–CHEESE.

MRS. ANNA OGIER.

Boil pig's feet till perfectly tender, so that the bones may be easily removed; season with pepper, salt stirred in; wet a mould in cold water, pour in the cheese, press down; when well formed, turn out, and keep in cornmeal gruel and vinegar.

FRENCH DEPARTMENT.

MEAT SOUP.

MADAME CHEVALLIER.

Take four pounds of meat and put in a soup pot filled with water; add a handful of salt. When the soup boils skim it; when no more scum rises, add two carrots, two turnips, celery, parsley, cloves, laurel leaf, some thyme and one onion, cut in four parts. Fill again the pot with water; keep a slow fire; let boil slowly, and leave on the fire for four hours.

————:o:————

POTATO SOUP.

MADAME CHEVALLIER.

Take three potatoes, one onion and some parsley; chopped, not too fine; put in a pot with piece of butter, brown well; add water and meat gravy, if you have any, and one spoonful of rice. Cook for two hours; salt and pepper to taste.

————:o:————

BLANQUETTE DE VEAU.

MADAME CHEVALLIER.

Take the breast of veal or lamb and cut in small pieces, melt a piece of butter the size of an egg; mix with it a large spoonful of flour; do not let brown. Add to this some boiling water, parsley, laurel and thyme, and place in a vessel with the veal; cook for two hours over a slow fire. Before serving, take the yolk of an egg and mix with it, stirring well.

————:o:————

CABBAGE SOUP.

MADAME CHEVALLIER.

Take one pound of pork (salt) and half of a cabbage-head; put the pork in a pot of cold water, let it boil for an hour; after which, throw the water off, replacing with hot water; when it boils, add the cabbage, carrot, turnip, and a piece of garlic, mashed with a knife, and pepper—*no salt;* let it boil for two hours, then take the cabbage out, put in a dish with the carrots and turnips around, the pork over it, and serve as a vegetable. Take the soup and pour into a dish over small pieces of bread.

————:o:————

MASHED PEA SOUP.

MADAME CHEVALLIER.

Soak for twenty-four hours one pound of pease, then put on the fire in cold water, with one onion, one clove and one laurel leaf, salt and pepper; boil for two hours; then strain and mash the pease; put them in the same water, with a piece of butter; cook half an hour. Take bread, cut in small pieces, and fry in butter to a light brown; put it in the soup dish, and when ready to serve, pour over the soup.

————:o:————

ONION SOUP.

MADAME CHEVALLIER.

Put in a pot some chopped onions and a piece of butter; when well browned, take a spoonful of flour and mix in. Pour into the pot, while stirring, one quart of milk; boil fifteen minutes; salt and pepper. Take the yolk of an egg, beat it with a little of the soup, and mix all together, stirring constantly. Pour the soup over slices of bread, cut very thin.

————:o:————

PUMPKIN SOUP.

MADAME CHEVALLIER.

Take two slices of pumpkin, wash, peel, and cut in small pieces; put in pot of water to boil; when cooked, empty out the water and strain the pumpkin; put in a pot, add water, one spoonful of rice or vermicelli, and a lump of butter; salt and pepper. When the rice is cooked the soup is done.

————:o:————

MUTTON STEW.

MADAME CHEVALLIER.

Chop some onion and fry; add a few potatoes, cut in small pieces, fry, then add small pieces of mutton, and when all is well fried, add water, cook for one hour and a half, then add a little parsley.

————:o:————

TOMATO SAUCE.

MADAME CHEVALLIER.

Take twelve tomatoes, an onion, a green pepper, parsley and garlic, let it cook for half an hour without water, then strain; afterwards add a piece of butter, with a small spoonful of flour; let it cook again for half an hour.

————:o:————

TURKEY STUFFING.

MADAME CHEVALLIER.

Chop an onion with some parsley, put in a pan with bread soaked in milk, one raw egg, and a large piece of butter; pepper and salt, fry for ten minutes, and then put it in the turkey, and sew the turkey up. If you wish olives in it, do not put in any onion.

————:o:————

COFFEE.

MADAME CHEVALLIER.

Use a French coffee pot; take half Java and half Costa Rica; filling the measure with coffee, throw over it boiling water until the coffee pot is full.

————:o:————

CHICKEN FRICASSEE.

MADAME CHEVALLIER.

Take the chicken, cut in pieces, and fry; then take an onion, chop, and fry until well browned; mix flour with it; add water, salt and pepper; put the chicken in with this, and let it cook for an hour with a slow fire.

————:o:————

HOW TO COOK EGGS.

MADAME MEYER.

Either poach or boil them not quite hard; make a to-mato sauce by cooking tomatoes in a good deal of butter; season with pepper and salt and add the yolks of two eggs, stirring the tomatoes slowly into the eggs; when this sauce is done pour it over the eggs.

————:o:————

FILLED EGGS.

MADAME MEYER.

Boil the eggs quite hard, then cut them across the centre, taking out the yolks; moisten some bread-crumbs with milk, squeeze them quite dry, mix them with the yolks well; to this add finely chopped parsley, and salt.

When this filling is well worked together, fill the whites with it; butter a flat pan, put the eggs in with the flat side down, and put whatever of the filling may be left over around them; make a rich white sauce, and pour it over them, sprinkle a few bread-crumbs over it, and set in the oven ten minutes. Dish it in the pan.

———:o:———

SAUTE—CHICKEN OR KIDNEY.

MADAME MEYER.

Slice and brown the chicken in fat; when nicely browned add a glass of soup, one onion, a carrot, some thyme and parsley, a small piece of garlic and one small green onion; let it cook for a little while; then add mushrooms and cook an hour or so longer; if you like, add a little chopped parsley.

———:o:———

MARANGOT — CHICKEN, LEG OF LAMB, OR RABBIT.

MADAME MEYER.

(Mushrooms with the chicken or leg of lamb, but not with rabbit.) Carve the same as you do for the Saute, and brown in sweet oil; then add pepper, salt and mushrooms; before adding the mushrooms to the marangot, brown them. When it is done, add a little tomato sauce, and decorate with toasted bread or fried eggs. In both of the above recipes you cut the meat or fowl the same as for any stew.

———:o:———

ESTRAGON—CHICKEN.

MADAME MEYER.

Scald the estragon (estragon is an herb). Take the liver of the chicken, chop it very fine, adding pepper and salt and a piece of butter. To this add the estragon and work them well together; then fill the chicken with it, and put it in the oven, with butter and a little lard, until it is nicely browned; after it is nicely browned you wrap it in white cooking paper; baste it very often until it is done. For the sauce, chop some estragon fine, add a little butter and flour; after they are well mixed, the yolk of one egg, a little soup, pepper and salt to taste, and just a little vinegar.

————:o:————

HOW TO STEW PIGEONS.

MADAME MEYER.

To a dozen pigeons take a bottle of olives, cut them as well as you can from the stones, and chop very fine with the livers of the pigeons; add bread crumbs, and season with thyme, ginger, pepper and salt; stuff the pigeons with this mixture and sew them up; rub some seasoning into them and wrap in grape leaves, so as to completely cover each one; then set aside. Brown some flour in a large lump of butter in a stew pan, and add some soup; put the pigeons in and stew till done; take off the grape leaves and dish.

POULTRY AND GAME.

HUNTERS' STEW.

J. A. GRAVES.

Let those who would partake of a delightful repast prepare—"*Ponen signa novis præceptis.*"

Take one dozen quail (use doves if you can't get quail), clean well, place them in a porcelain lined stew pan, with tight fitting cover. Let the pan be large enough to admit of all additions hereinafter enumerated. Pour in a gallon of water; add two pods of red pepper, black pepper and salt, to suit taste, and small slice of bacon; boil well with cover on for at least an hour; then add potatoes, tomatoes, one large onion, quartered, celery, chopped fine, green corn, cut from the ear (canned corn, if fresh is not in season), two table spoonfuls of fresh butter, more water, if necessary to keep from burning, and stew for at least an hour and a half. Regulate the amount of vegetables according to taste. The tomatoes and corn add much to the flavor. A few rabbits, quartered and cooked with the birds, is also an improvement. Serve hot.

————:o:————

TO FATTEN A TURKEY, MAKE THE DRESSING AND ROAST IT.

MRS. ANNA OGIER.

Get your turkey six weeks before you need it; put him in a coop just large enough to let him walk, or in a small yard; give him walnuts—one the first day, and increase every day one till he has nine; then go back to one and up to nine until you kill him, stuffing him twice with corn meal dough each day, in which put a little chopped onion and celery, if you have it. For the dressing, use bread, picked up fine, a table spoonful of butter, some sage, thyme, chopped onion, pepper, salt, and the yolks of two eggs, and pour in a little boiling water to make it stick together; before putting it in the turkey pour boiling water inside and outside, to cleanse and plump it; then roast it in a tin kitchen, basting all the time. It will be splendid, served with a nice piece of ham and cranberry sauce.

————:o:————

TO COOK SPRING CHICKEN.

MRS. C. G. DU BOIS.

Separate each joint; after cleansing and washing, dry in a towel; melt equal portions of butter and lard; when hot, fry the pieces carefully and place them in a covered dish. Turn the drippings out of the pan, put in a spoonful of butter. When melted, pour in a teacup of cream which has salt and pepper, a little grated nutmeg and a little parsley in; stir it well, and when it boils pour over the chicken.

————:o:————

SMOTHERED CHICKEN.

MRS. GEORGE CLARK.

Prepare a fowl as for roasting, put it in a pot of boiling water and cook until tender; within twenty minutes of being done add a cup of rice, which will cook in the gravy; add parsley, pepper and salt. Serve the chicken in a dish with the rice around it.

————:o:————

JELLIED CHICKEN.

MRS. J. G. HOWARD.

Boil a chicken (or chickens) in as little water as possible until the meat falls from the bones; chop the meat fine, seasoning with a little salt, pepper, lemon or mace; put into the bottom of a mold some slices of hard-boiled eggs, then a layer of chopped chicken, another of egg, then chicken, until the mold is nearly full. Boil down the water in which the chicken was cooked, with a large piece of gelatine or sea-moss farina, until about a cup and a half is left; season and strain through a very coarse net, and pour over the mold of chicken. Let it stand over night, or all day, near the ice; to be garnished with celery tops or parsley.

———:o:———

FRIED CHICKEN.

MRS. I. W. HELLMAN.

Cut the chicken in quarters, cut out the bones, without spoiling the shape of the chicken, lay them in a bowl with vinegar and a very little sweet oil, season with pepper, salt, a few young onions, parsely and thyme; let remain this way for a few hours, turning it in the meanwhile several times; then take out and dry on a towel; dip the pieces in a batter composed of flour, eggs and water. Fry nice and brown.

———:o:———

PRESSED CHICKEN OR FOWL.

MRS. M. G. MOORE.

Take the meat from the bones of a cooked fowl, chop fine, season highly, add to it dressing and gravy; heat hot, stirring all the while, then put into a mold, laying a heavy weight upon it; when cold, slice it.

———:o:———

BREAKFAST QUAIL.

J. A. GRAVES.

Prepare the birds by opening on the back; put them in a dripping pan; season well with salt, pepper and a generous supply of butter; add enough water to cover the bottom of the pan; then place your pan in a hot oven and frequently turn your birds, and baste them with the seasoned water in the pan, which gradually cooks down and makes a fine gravy. By continued basting, your birds, when well done and nicely browned, will still be rich and juicy, and will be of much better flavor than when broiled. Serve on thin slices of buttered toast.

————:o:————

PRESSED CHICKEN.

MRS. J. W. GILLETTE.

Put two chickens in a pot, cover with water, and stew slowly until the meat drops from the bone, then take out and chop it. Let the liquor boil down until there is a cupful; put in a small cup of butter, a table spoonful of salt, one of pepper, a little parsley and a beaten egg; stir this through the meat; Slice a hard-boiled egg, lay in the dish, and press in the meat; when ready for the table garnish with celery tops.

————:o:————

YOUNG CHICKEN WITH CAULIFLOWER.

MRS. I. W. HELLMAN.

Cut the chicken in pieces and boil in water seasoned with different spices and a little lemon juice, thickened with a little flour and the yolks of several eggs; cook the cauliflower in water, with a little salt and butter; after it is cooked tender, drain it. Serve the chicken in the center of a dish, surrounded by the cauliflower, and pour the gravy over all.

————:o:————

CHICKEN STEW.

MRS. C. G. DU BOIS.

Cut up two tender chickens; cover with lukewarm water and boil gently until done; salt the liquor to taste; when the chicken is cooked remove to a dish and keep warm. Take the pot from the fire and skim the grease from the liquor, then place the pot of liquor over the fire; mix well together half teacup of sifted flour, two well beaten eggs and half teacup of milk; add some of the liquor; then pour all into the boiling liquor, stirring all the time; salt and pepper; put the chicken in, let it boil up once, then remove to a large dish.

————:o:————

TURKEY STUFFING.

MRS. R. M. WIDNEY.

Take stale but very light sweet bread, pour over cold water, and drain as dry as possible immediately; let stand an hour or more, then add butter plentifully, pepper, salt, sage, and lastly, chestnuts which have been previously boiled in salt water, peeled and chopped.

————:o:————

TO COOK WILD DUCKS.

MRS. C. G. DU BOIS.

Put the ducks in a large pot, cover with cold water, and add two good sized onions for each duck; when half done remove from the water, stuff with mashed potato and beaten egg—two to each fowl—seasoned with onions, sage, salt and pepper, and bake until thoroughly done, frequently basting with gravy. Serve with brown gravy, in which is stirred parsley, chopped fine and fried in butter.

————:o:————

TOUGH OLD FOWLS.

MRS. JOHN SMITH.

Make a stuffing of bread crumbs, celery and butter, chopped and mixed; salt and pepper to taste; stuff the fowl and sew up the openings with coarse thread; when it is ready to cook, lay the fowl on a wire tea stand in a pot and put in about a quart of water; cover very closely; the fowl must not be in the water, but above it; put the pot over a slow fire and let it boil very slowly for two to three hours, depending on the age and toughness of the fowl; when tender put in a baking pan with the water, which should be much reduced by this time, and bake for twenty minutes or half an hour—long enough to brown nicely. If the fowl is fat, as it should be, this is a sure way of making it eatable.

———- :o:———

TO ROAST TEAL DUCKS.

MRS. ANNA OGIER.

Pick and clean and hang them for two days; make a stuffing of bread, picked up; salt, pepper, onions and a small piece of butter; put them into a pan and dredge them with flour, a little pepper and salt; baste frequently.

———:o:———

BOILED FOWL WITH OYSTERS.

MRS. GEORGE CLARK.

Take a young fowl, stuff with oysters, put it into a jar, and plunge the jar in a kettle of water; boil for an hour and a half; there will be a quantity of gravy from the juices of the fowl and oysters, in the jar; make it into a white sauce with the addition of an egg and some cream, or a little flour and some butter; add oysters to it, or serve it plain with the fowl. The gravy that comes from a fowl dressed in this manner will be a stiff jelly the next day, while the fowl will be very white and tender and of an exceedingly fine flavor.

———:o:———

PRESSED CHICKEN.

MRS. L. M. THOMPSON.

Boil the chicken until the meat drops from the bones, remove from the pot and shred fine, season with pepper, salt and a little butter. Let the liquor left in the pot boil down, so as to leave not more than a small teacupful; pour it on the chicken and stir in. Dip a mold in cold water and fill with the chicken; press down and let stand over night. Serve with Saratoga potatoes.

———:o:———

ROAST TURKEY.

MRS. T. S. STANWAY.

Wash the inside and outside of the turkey. Prepare a dressing in the following manner: Soak sufficient bread in cold water to fill the turkey. Add half cup of melted butter. season with salt, pepper, sage, nutmeg or mace, thyme or marjoram. One egg in the dressing makes it cut smoothly. Fill the crop and body with dressing, sew up, tie the legs and wings, rub well with butter and a little salt; dredge with flour; roast it from two to four hours, according to size. It should roast slowly at first and be basted frequently, having two-thirds of a pint of water in the dripping pan. Boil the liver and gizzard, mince fine, thicken the gravy with a little flour, and add a spoonful of currant jelly if liked.

———:o:———

ANOTHER WAY TO COOK DUCKS OF A LARGE SIZE.

MRS. ANNA OGIER.

Stuff them with oysters and bread, put them in a pot with a little water and steam till done.

———:o:———

ROAST GOOSE.

MRS. T. S. STANWAY.

A goose for roasting should be young, tender and fat. In preparing a goose for cooking, save the giblets for the gravy. After the goose has been drawn, singed well, washed and wiped inside and out, and trussed so as to look round and short, make a quantity of stuffing of dry bread crumbs, three good-sized onions, minced fine, sage, pepper and salt, one egg, two if the goose is large, and three spoonfuls of butter. Fill the goose and roast; keep well basted. A goose must be thoroughly done. Roast from two to three hours, according to size. Boil the giblets in water, seasoned with salt, pepper and a bit of butter, dredged with flour. Mince liver and gizzard fine; put the two gravies together and serve them up in a gravy tureen. To serve with goose, have apple sauce, made of fine Jersey apples, steamed very dry and well sweetened.

———:o:———

BONED TURKEY.

MRS. ADELIA HALL.

Boil a turkey in as little water as possible until the meat falls from the bones. Remove all the bones and skin. Pick the meat into small pieces and mix light and dark together. Season with pepper, salt and sage; put into a mold and pour the liquor over, which must be kept warm; press with a heavy weight.

———:o:———

PLOVERS.

MRS. T. S. STANWAY.

Birds with peculiar and pleasant flavor. Roast plain, basting only with butter, or fill them with a forcemeat and rub over the outside with beaten egg, and then roll each plover in finely-grated bread crumbs and roast. Serve upon buttered toast.

———:o:———

SMOTHERED CHICKEN.

MRS. ADELIA HALL.

Dress chickens and let them stand in water half an hour, to make white; put in a baking pan, first cutting them open at the back; sprinkle salt and pepper over them, putting a piece of butter here and there. Then cover tightly with another pan the same size and bake one hour. Baste often with butter.

———:o:———

BIRDS WITH MUSHROOMS.

MRS. T. S. STANWAY.

Take plovers, woodcock or snipe; truss them as if for roasting; put into each a button mushroom. Have a quart of mushrooms; put the birds and remaining mushrooms into a stew pan; season with a little salt and pepper; add a quarter of a pound of butter, rolled in flour, with a little water. If cream is plentiful you may use half cream and half butter. Cover the pan closely and stew gently till the birds and mushrooms are tender all through. Dip in hot water slices of toast with the crust trimmed off. When the birds are done lay them on the toast, with the mushrooms around. If you cannot get button mushrooms, divide large ones into quarters.

———:o:———

CHICKEN SANDWICHES.

MRS. ADELIA HALL.

Stew a chicken until very tender; season with a little salt; take out the bones and pack the meat firmly in a deep dish, mixing white and dark meat nicely together; pour the broth in which the chicken was stewed over it. There should be just enough to cover the meat nicely. When cold cut in smooth slices; if desired, sprinkle with marjoram or sage, and place between slices of good bread.

———:o:———

FORCEMEAT STUFFING.

MRS. T. S. STANWAY.

Forcemeat is considered an indispensable accompaniment to most made dishes, and when composed with good taste gives additional spirit and relish to even that "sovereign of savoriness," turtle soup. It is also sent up in patties, and for stuffing veal, game, poultry, etc. The ingredients should be so proportioned that no one flavor predominates. To give the same flavor to the stuffing of poultry, game, or veal, etc., argues a poverty of invention. With a little contrivance you may make as great a variety as you have dishes. The poignancy of forcemeat or stuffing should be proportioned to the savoriness of the viands to which it is intended to give an additional zest. Some dishes require a very delicately flavored forcemeat. For others it must be full and highly seasoned. What would be fine for turkey would be insipid for roast pig. Most people have an acquired and peculiar taste in stuffing, etc., and what exactly pleases one seldom is what another considers the most agreeable. The consistency of forcemeats is rather a difficult thing to manage. Take care to have the ingredients fine and thoroughly incorporated. Forcemeat balls must not be larger than a small nutmeg. If they are for brown sauce, flour and fry them; if for white, put them into boiling water and boil them for three minutes. The latter are by far the most delicate. Sweetbreads and tongues are the favorite materials for forcemeat. No one flavor should predominate. A selection may be made from the following list, being careful to use the least of those articles which are the most pungent: Cold fowl, veal, ham, game, fat bacon, beef suet, crumbs of bread, parsley, white pepper, salt, nutmeg, yolks and whites of eggs, well beaten, to bind the mixture. The forcemeat may be made with any of these articles without any striking flavor. Therefore any of the following different ingredients may be made use of to vary the taste: Oysters, tarragon, savory, sage, thyme, marjoram, sweet basil, garlic, cayenne, onions, mace, cloves, and yolks of hard-boiled eggs and curry powder.

------:o:------

BROILED QUAIL.

MRS. ADELIA HALL.

Dress carefully, and soak a short time in salt and water. Split down the back; dry with a cloth, and rub them over with butter; place on the gridiron over a clear fire; turn often, and dip in melted butter; season with salt. Prepare a slice of thin toast, nicely buttered and laid on a hot dish, for each bird. Lay a bird breast upward on each piece. Garnish with currant jelly.

VEGETABLE DEPARTMENT.

OLD VIRGINIA CORN PUDDING.

MRS. ANNA OGIER.

Cut and scrape one dozen ears of corn; place in a yellow dish which it will nearly fill; break into this two eggs. When thoroughly beaten with the corn, add two tablespoonfuls of flour, a teaspoonful of salt, half teaspoonful of black pepper; mix all well together; fill the pan with milk, stirring it very carefully into the corn, and when it is mixed put small bits of butter over the top and bake about half an hour. If the corn is not sweet corn, some add to the other ingredients one teaspoonful of sugar.

———:o:———

SPINACH.

MRS. R. M. WIDNEY.

Wash and pick your spinach very carefully; drop into boiling water and cook fifteen minutes. Drain thoroughly through a colander; then chop quite fine. Return to the stove; add one tablespoonful of butter; pepper and salt to taste. Put in vegetable dish and garnish with hard-boiled eggs.

———:o:———

TO COOK CABBAGE.

MRS. E. F. SPENCE.

Take a nice, firm, medium-sized cabbage; wash; cut in four pieces. Have on a kettle with boiling water, in which is salt and one eighth of a teaspoonful of soda; put in the cabbage and boil twenty-five minutes. Serve hot.

————:o:————

CABBAGE PUDDING.

MRS. E. WORKMAN.

Half head of cabbage, chopped fine and scalded in boiling water. Drain and mix with it four well beaten eggs, two cupfuls sweet cream, two tablespoonfuls melted butter, four biscuit, crumbled, salt and pepper; stir well and bake in a dish.

————:o:————

STEWED TOMATOES.

MRS. C. G. DU BOIS.

Pour scalding water over your tomatoes, and as soon as the skin seems loosened pour off again; peel and cut up into a porcelain-lined stew pan. Let them boil some thirty minutes, and just a few minutes before taking up add butter, salt and pepper to taste. Sugar, cracker, bread or flour destroys the pure flavor of the tomato.

————:o:————

EXCELLENT BAKED POTATOES.

MRS. M. G. MOORE.

One quart peeled potatoes, sliced thin; one cup of cream; pepper and salt. Bake one hour in a pudding dish. Serve hot.

————:o:————

OLD-FASHIONED SLAW.

MRS. MARY A. LINDLEY.

Piece of butter the size of an egg, half a teacup of vinegar, one of sweet cream, one egg, heaped tablespoonful of sugar. Put the butter and vinegar in a skillet and heat; mix egg, cream and sugar together and stir slowly into the heated vinegar. Have the cabbage chopped or cut, and sprinkle with salt and pepper; put it into the mixture and let it scald for a minute or two.

————:o:————

SARSA OF TOMATOES.

MRS. M. E. J.

Take one quart of tomatoes, six or eight pods of green peppers, and two onions; chop together; add salt and a little butter; stew slowly. To this may be added any kind of chopped meat desired.

————:o:————

BAKED BEANS.

MRS. C. G. DU BOIS.

One pint of beans, parboiled till the skins crack when blown upon. Pour off the water and place the beans in your dish or pot. Take a piece of salt pork about two inches square; wash it clean; slit the skin and place in the middle of the beans so all is covered save the skin. Dissolve a tablespoonful of sugar in as much water as will cover the beans, and pour over them. Bake three or four hours.

————:o:————

YOUNG CORN OMELET.

MRS. GEO. CLARK.

To a dozen ears of fine young corn allow five eggs. Boil the corn a quarter of an hour, and then with a large grater grate it down from the cob. Beat the eggs very light, and then stir gradually the grated corn into the pan of eggs. Add a small saltspoon of salt, a very little cayenne. Put into a frying-pan equal quantities of butter and fresh lard; stir them well together over the fire. When they boil, put in this mixture thick, and fry it, afterwards browning the top with a red-hot shovel or a salamander. Transfer it, when done, to a heated dish, but do not fold it over. It will be found excellent. This is a good way of using boiled corn that has been left from dinner the preceding day.

————:o:————

STRINGED BEANS.

MRS. R. M. WIDNEY.

After stringing, washing, and snapping beans into small pieces, cover with cold water and cook until perfectly tender. If water remains turn it off. Cook dry being careful not to burn. Then add one tablespoon of butter; stir for a moment or two, after which add salt, pepper and cream; half a teacup will do; more is better.

————:o:————

ASPARAGUS.

MRS. ANNA OGIER.

Boil tender in salted water, and serve with melted butter.

————:o:————

IMITATION OYSTERS.

MRS. MARY A. LINDLEY.

Grate young green corn in a dish. To one pint of grated corn add one egg, well beaten, a small teacup of flour, half a cup of butter. Season with salt and pepper; mix well together. A tablespoonful of the mixture will equal an oyster in size. Fry a light brown, and when done butter them.

————:o:————

CORN PUDDING.

MRS. GOODWIN.

Cut the corn lengthwise and scrape out the juices. Fill the buttered dish two-thirds full of corn; add one-third of milk, to which has been added two well-beaten eggs. Stir this mixture, season with pepper and salt, and butter in bits on top.

————:o:————

OKRA.

MRS. ANNA OGIER.

Boil in clear water, with a little salt. When tender, dish and season with butter, pepper and salt.

————:o:————

EGG PLANTS.

MRS. M. E. J.

Boil three or four large ones till tender. Peel and mash. Season with black pepper, salt, and a teaspoonful of thyme; add a little butter and a few bread crumbs. Mold in a pie pan, sprinkle bread crumbs on top, and lay a few dabs of butter around. Brown in the oven.

————:o:————

BAKED TOMATOES FOR BREAKFAST.

MRS. T. S. STANWAY.

Take a quart of cold stewed tomatoes, beat into it two eggs, four tablespoonfuls of bread crumbs, a tablespoonful of chopped parsley, a little more salt and pepper, and bake for twenty minutes in a quick oven.

————:o:————

BAKED BEANS.

MRS. MARY BACKMAN.

One quart of white beans, soaked over night. Put on two quarts of water; boil one hour. Put in a piece of corned pork, about one pound—a thin piece; boil a half hour in with the beans. Then take out the beans and pork; put them in a dish, to bake in the oven. Place the pork in the center of the beans and score well. Pour two tablespoonfuls of molasses over the beans.

———:o:———

FRIED TOMATOES FOR BREAKFAST.

MRS. T. S. STANWAY.

Take large, smooth tomatoes, cut them in slices, one-half inch thick; dip them in powdered bread-crumbs, and fry them a light brown, in half lard and half butter.

———:o:———

TO BOIL CORN.

MRS. T. S. STANWAY.

Put it in boiling water. Never allow it to boil over five minutes; after that it becomes hard and tough.

———:o:———

PARSNIPS.

MRS. M. E. J.

Boil, mash, season with butter, pepper and salt, and make into little cakes; roll in flour and brown in hot lard.

———:o:———

MACARONI—ITALIAN STYLE.

LOUISEJ.

Break macaroni in three-inch lengths and put in boiling salt water, and boil twenty-five minutes. Then drain and dress with following sauce: Take two pounds of lean beef; without any fat, and stew gently with a small cup of cold water until the juice is entirely extracted. Chop an onion very fine; cut up two tomatoes and three or four mushrooms; add pepper and salt, and stew in the beef juice until you are ready to dish the macaroni. First sprinkle your dish with grated Parmesan cheese; then add a layer of macaroni, over which pour some sauce. Fill the dish in this order, having macaroni with sauce on top.

————:o:————

ASPARAGUS.

MRS. T. S. STANWAY.

Trim off the tough part of the stalks, tie in small bundles, and boil it fifteen to twenty minutes. Toast some bread and dip it in the water in which the asparagus was cooked. Then lay a bundle of asparagus on each slice of toast. Make drawn butter and turn it over the whole.

————:o:————

FRIED TOMATOES.

MRS. I. S. MAYO.

Cut ripe tomatoes in two, and fry slowly on both sides, in butter or lard. When thoroughly cooked, take them out, pour a little milk or cream in the frying-pan, thicken with a little flour, and season with salt and a pinch of red pepper; pour it over the tomatoes, and serve.

————:o:————

CORN OYSTERS.

MRS. T. S. STANWAY.

Grate twelve ears of sweet corn; add two well-beaten eggs, a pinch of salt and two teaspoonfuls of white sugar. Drop in hot lard and fry until done.

————:o:————

RICE AND CHEESE.

MRS. M. E. J.

Put a layer of rice boiled in milk in the bottom of a buttered pudding dish; grate upon it some rich, mild cheese, and scatter over it some bits of butter. Spread upon the cheese more rice, and fill the dish in this order, having rice at the top, buttered well, without the cheese. Add a few spoonfuls of cream or milk and a very little salt. Cover and bake half an hour. Then brown nicely, and serve in the bake-dish.

————:o:————

GREEN PEASE.

MRS. T. S. STANWAY.

To one quart of pease put a tablespoonful of white sugar. When cooked, drain them dry, and add butter, salt and pepper to your taste. If liked, use cream instead of butter.

————:o:————

CHEESE OMELET.

MRS. GEORGE CLARK.

It is necessary to have a rather small frying-pan to have good omelets, for if a large one is used the ingredients will spread over it and become thin. Another rule to observe is, that omelets should be fried only on one side. Use from five to ten eggs, according to the sized dish required. Break them up singly and carefully, each one to be well and separately beaten or whisked. Add to them grated cheese, the quantity to be regulated according to the number of eggs used—three ounces to four eggs; salt and pepper to the taste. Dissolve in a small, clean frying-pan about an ounce of butter; pour in the ingredients, and as soon as the omelet is well risen and appears quite firm (from five to seven minutes with a good fire), fold it over and slide it carefully onto a hot dish. Place it in the oven for one minute. Do not let it stand before serving.

————:o:————

FRENCH, OR STRING BEANS.

MRS. T. S. STANWAY.

String the beans and cut off the ends. Cut them very small. To one pound and a half of beans take one tomato, peeled, a very small quantity of onion and two Chilleis. Remove the seeds and chop fine, and add a large lump of butter and salt and pepper. When nearly cooked, add one tablespoonful of vinegar, and one-half. spoonful of flour, made smooth in a little water. Let it come to a boil, and dish up. Use only enough water to cook them.

———:o:———

IRISH POTATOES, FRIED.

MRS. T. S. STANWAY.

Take raw potatoes, peel them, slice them very thin, pour cold water over them, and let them stand one hour or more; drain off the water, dry them in a napkin, and throw them into boiling lard. When cooked, skim them out into a hot dish and sprinkle a little salt over them.

———:o:———

MACARONI.

MRS. M. E. J.

One-half pound of macaroni in long pieces. Soak fifteen minutes in warm water; drain and put in a saucepan; pour over it a half pint of meat gravy, with some shreds of meat in it; add three ounces of old cheese, two large tomatoes, and one clove of garlic, all chopped fine. Season well with red pepper and salt. Boil fifteen minutes, shaking it occasionally, but not stirring. When done, add a tablespoonful of butter and sprinkle two ounces of grated cheese over the top.

———:o:———

SUCCOTASH.

MRS. T. S. STANWAY.

Cut the corn from twelve ears. Take one-third the quantity of Lima beans. Put the beans to cook in water enough to cover them. Cook one-half hour; then add the corn, with a large spoonful of white sugar, a good-sized piece of butter, and salt and pepper to taste. In cutting the corn from the ears use a sharp knife; cut only half of the kernel. This is added to the beans. Then take a knife and scrape the corn clean from the ears. Set this to one side. A few moments before dishing up the succotash, add the corn or milk taken from the ears last. Stir it well, as it will burn very easily afterwards.

————:o:————

SWEET POTATOES, FRIED.

MRS. T. S. STANWAY.

Pour boiling water over them; half cook them, drain off the water, peel them, cut in slices half an inch thick, and fry in batter to a nice brown.

————:o:————

IRISH POTATOES, STEWED.

MRS. T. S. STANWAY.

Put into a saucepan two ounces of butter and one table-spoonful of flour; stir smooth. Add some parsley, chopped fine, salt and pepper, and stir up together. Then add a cup of rich milk. Set it on the fire, stirring continually until it boils. Cut some cold boiled potatoes in long, narrow strips or slices and put them in the saucepan. Let them boil up, and serve hot.

SAUCE DEPARTMENT.

———:o:———

MAYONNAISE SAUCE.

MRS. HENDERSON'S COOK BOOK.

Put the uncooked yolk of an egg into a cold bowl; beat
it well with a silver fork; then add two salt-spoonfuls of
salt and one salt-spoonful of mustard powder; work them
well a minute before adding the oil; then mix in a little
good oil, which must be poured in very slowly (a few drops
at a time) at first, alternated occasionally with a few drops
of vinegar. In proportion as the oil is used, the sauce
should gain consistency. When it begins to have the appearance of jelly, alternate a few drops of lemon juice with
the oil. When the egg has absorbed a gill of oil, finish the
sauce by adding a very little pinch of cayenne pepper and
one and a half teaspoonfuls of good vinegar. Taste it to
see that there are salt, mustard, cayenne and vinegar enough.
If not, add more very carefully. These proportions will
suit most tastes; yet some like more mustard and more oil.
Be cautious not to use too much cayenne.

By beating the egg a minute before adding the oil,
there is little danger of the sauce curdling; yet if, by adding
too much oil at first, it should possibly curdle, immediately
interrupt the operation. Put the yolks of one or two eggs
on another plate; beat them well, and add the curdled Mayonnaise by degrees, and finish by adding more oil, lemon
juice, vinegar, salt, and cayenne according to taste. If
lemons are not at hand, many use vinegar instead.

Delmonico uses four yolks of eggs for two quart bottles
of oil. It is only necessary, then, to use one yolk for a pint
of oil, the egg only being a foundation for the sauce. It is

easier, however, to begin with more yolks; many use three of them for a gill of oil. The sauce will not curdle so easily if the few drops of vinegar are used at first, after a very little oil is used. It keeps perfectly well by putting it into a glass preserve or pickle bottle, with a ground-glass stopper. It is well to have enough made to last a week at least. The opportunity of making. it may be taken, and adding it to the Mayonnaise bottle, when there are extra yolks left after the whites of the eggs are used for other purposes, such as white cake, corn-starch, pudding, etc.

It requires about a quarter of an hour to make this sauce. In summer the process of making it is greatly facilitated by placing the eggs and oil in the ice-chest half an hour before using them.

————:o:————

TOMATOES A' LA MAYONNAISE.

MRS. HENDERSON'S COOK BOOK.

This is truly a delicious dish; it would, in fact, be good every day during the tomato season.

Select large, fine tomatoes and place them in the ice-chest; the colder they are the better, if not frozen. Skin them without the use of hot water and slice them, still retaining the form of the whole tomato. Arrange them in uniform order on a dish, with a spoonful of Mayonnaise sauce thick as a jelly on the top of each tomato. Garnish the dish with leaves of any kind. Parsley is very pretty.

Some marinate the tomato slices, *i. e.*, dip them into a mixture of three spoonfuls of vinegar to one spoonful of oil, pepper, and salt; and then, after draining well, mix them in the Mayonnaise sauce.

————:o:————

CHICKEN SALAD.

MRS. HENDERSON'S COOK BOOK.

Boil a young tender chicken, and when cold, separate the meat from the bones; cut it into little square blocks or dice; do not mince it. Cut white tender stalks of celery into about three-quarter-inch lengths, saving the outside green stalks for soups. Mix the chicken and celery together, and then stir well into them a mixture in the proportion of three tablespoonfuls of vinegar to one tablespoonful of oil, with pepper, salt, and a little mustard to taste. Put this aside for an hour or two, or until just before serving. This is called marinating the chicken; it will absorb the vinegar, etc. When about to serve, mix the celery and chicken with a Mayonnaise sauce, leaving a portion of the sauce to mask the top. Reserve several fresh ends or leaves of celery with which to garnish the dish. Stick a little bouquet of these tops in the center of the salad, then a row of them around it. From the center to each of the four sides sprinkle rows of capers. Sometimes slices or little cut diamonds of hard-boiled eggs are used for garnishing.

Chicken salad is often made with lettuce instead of celery. Marinate the chicken alone; add it to the small tender leaves (uncut) of the lettuce the last moment before serving; then pour Mayonnaise dressing over the top. Garnish with little center-heads of lettuce, capers, cold chopped red beets if you choose, or sliced hard boiled eggs. Sometimes little strips of anchovy are added for a garnish. When on the table it should all be mixed together. Many may profit by this recipe for chicken salad, for it is astonishing how few understand making so common a dish. It is generally minced, and mixed with hard-boiled eggs, etc., for a dress-.ing.

————:o:————

SALAD DRESSING.

MRS. J. E. HOLLENBECK.

Beat yolks of eight eggs, add to them a cup of sugar, one tablespoonful each of salt, mustard, and black pepper, a little cayenne pepper, and half a cupful of cream; mix thoroughly. Bring to a boil a pint and a half of vinegar; add one cupful of butter, and boil again; pour upon the mixture, and stir it well. It can be kept for weeks by bottling when cold, and putting away in a cool place.

ANOTHER:—Yolks of two hard-boiled eggs, rubbed very fine and smooth, one teaspoonful English mustard, one of salt, the yolks of two raw eggs beaten into the others, a dessertspoonful of fine sugar; add very fresh sweet oil, poured in by very small quantities, and beaten as long as the mixture continues to thicken; then add vinegar till as thin as desired; if not hot enough with mustard, add a little cayenne pepper.

————:o:————

CABBAGE SALAD.

MRS. J. M. STEWART.

One salad bowl cabbage, cut fine, three-quarter pint of vinegar, and lump of butter the size of a walnut; bring to a boil, then add one (or two, if the cabbage is watery,) well-beaten eggs, with one-half pint *rich* cream. One teaspoonful sugar, one-half teaspoonful salt, one-half teaspoonful corn-starch, one teaspoonful, grated dry, horse-radish, two pinches black pepper. Stir briskly until it boils, and mix with the cut cabbage while hot.

————:o:————

POTATO SALAD.

MRS. M. M. TEMPLETON.

Chop fine one small onion, slice then twelve cold pota-toes; season with pepper, salt, and three tablespoonfuls of vinegar, one of made mustard, two of salad oil; mix thor-oughly. A little chopped celery improves it.

————:o:————

POTATO SALAD.

MRS. J. E. HOLLENBECK.

Slice cold boiled potatoes fine, with enough fine sliced raw onions to season; add pepper, salt, sweet oil, and vine-gar to suit taste; mixing with care not to break slices of potatoes.

————:o:————

SALAD DRESSING.

MRS. J. DE BARTH SHORB.

For an ordinary salad of any kind for a family of six or eight persons.—To a teaspoonful of mustard add sufficient water to reduce to a paste about the consistence of batter; then add the yolks of two or three fresh eggs; beat the compound well until the ingredients are thoroughly mixed. Two teaspoonfuls of white sugar are then dissolved in the smallest quantity of water, and stirred into the mixture. Add a small quantity of red pepper (one-quarter of a teaspoonful). Pour in the oil, two tablespoonfuls at a time, mixing thoroughly in the dressing until ten or twelve tablespoonfuls of oil have been used. Finally add two tablespoonfuls of vinegar.

———:o:———

SALAD DRESSING.

MRS. S. SPEEDY. ·

Beat two eggs; add one-half teacup of vinegar, one teaspoonful of mustard, one of sugar, one-half teaspoonful of salt, and a lump of butter the size of a walnut. Set this in boiling water until the egg is cooked; stir constantly. This makes a very nice dressing, especially for cabbage.

———:o:———·

CHICKEN SALAD.

MRS. M. M. TEMPLETON.

Two large chickens, boiled; the yolks of nine hardboiled eggs, half pint of vinegar, one gill of mustard, mixed, one small teaspoonful of cayenne pepper, one teaspoonful of salt, and four large heads of celery, chopped fine.

———:o:———

SALAD DRESSING.

MRS. ANNA OGIER.

To two hard-boiled yolks of eggs, beaten well, add and incorporate one salt-spoonful of table salt, one mustard-spoonful of raw mustard, a teaspoonful of soft sugar, and one cayenne-spoonful of cayenne pepper. Before beginning, rub the basin over with a bit of garlic or onion. When all is well pounded, add very gently, mixing all the time, four tablespoonfuls of cream or milk and two tablespoonfuls of vinegar. The last must be put in slowly, as it depends on the strength of the vinegar how much to use. Stop pouring in when the dressing becomes thick. This dressing was taught me by an old epicure, and whenever I make it every one speaks of its perfection.

————:o:————

DRESSING FOR SALAD.

MRS. M. M. TEMPLETON.

One egg, one tablespoonful of cream, one tablespoonful of white sugar, three of vinegar, one of olive oil, one of mixed mustard, and a little salt.

————:o:————

CHICKEN SALAD.

MRS. J. E. HOLLENBECK.

One teaspoonful mustard, two hard-boiled yolks of eggs, well mashed, two raw yolks of eggs, well beaten, pepper and salt to taste, half a bottle of sweet oil, three tablespoonfuls of vinegar, celery and lettuce; breast of chicken; shred it; do not chop it.

————:o:————

SALAD DRESSING.

MISS TUTHILL.

The yolk of one hard-boiled egg, mashed very fine and smooth, one teaspoonful of sugar, one salt-spoon even full of salt, one-half teaspoonful of dry mustard, and two or three sprinkles of black pepper from the pepper-box. Mix the dry things all together with the mashed yolk; then add one raw yolk; mix in well with a wooden salad-spoon; then add a salad-spoonful and a half of oil, a little at a time; beat thoroughly, and then add two salad-spoonfuls of vinegar.

EGG DEPARTMENT.

——:o:——

SHIRRED EGGS.

MRS. S. C. HUBBELL.

Put a lump of butter in a tin plate or shallow pudding dish, and place on the stove till the butter is hissing hot; then put in the number of eggs desired, previously broken with care on a plate. Let them cook till the whites are partially set. Serve immediately, in the hot dish. They are to be seasoned to taste when eaten.

——:o:——

OMELET.

MRS. T. S. STANWAY.

Break the eggs in one dish; stir rather than beat them. To each three eggs add a spoonful of cold water; salt and pepper to taste. Put two ounces of butter in the pan. When the butter is hot, put in the omelet. As soon as cooked on one side, turn over quickly and cook on the other side. Serve on a very hot plate, and sprinkle a little chopped parsley over the top. " Water makes an omelet light, tender, and moist."

——:o:——

OMELET.

MRS. H. K. S. O'MELVENY.

Take six eggs, well beaten (the yolks and whites separately), a pint cupful of warm milk with a tablespoonful of butter melted in it, a tablespoonful of flour wet in a little cold milk, a teaspoonful of salt, and a little pepper. Mix all together, adding the whites of the eggs last. Cook immediately in a frying-pan on the top of the stove until baked on the bottom; then brown in the oven.

————:o:————

FRENCH EGGS.

MRS. E. WORKMAN.

Boil hard five eggs; boil three onions; chop both fine; add a spoonful of butter, three biscuit, broken fine, and salt and pepper to taste. Stir well together and bake in a dish.

————:o:————

BAKED OMELET.

MRS. M. MCLELLAN.

Heat three gills of milk with a dessert spoonful of butter in it. Beat four or five eggs thoroughly. Mix a tablespoonful of flour with a teaspoonful of salt; smooth in a little cold milk; mix the eggs with the flour and cold milk; then add the hot milk, stirring fast. Bake fifteen or twenty minutes in a buttered dish in a quick oven.

————:o:————

OMELET.

MRS. A. A. DODSWORTH.

Six eggs, one cup of milk, one tablespoonful of flour, and a pinch of salt. Beat the whites and yolks separately; mix the flour, milk, and salt; add the yolks, and then the beaten whites. Have a buttered dish very hot; pour in; bake in a quick oven five minutes. A perfect omelet.

————:o:————

CURRIED EGGS.

MRS. M. E. J.

Slice an onion; fry brown; add a tablespoonful of curry powder, a pint of good broth, and a little salt; let it cook till the onion is tender. Thicken a half pint of milk with cornstarch, and stir in; let it simmer a few minutes; then add a dozen hard-boiled eggs, halved; warm through. Take the eggs up and arrange in a dish and pour the gravy over.

————:o:————

OMELET SOUFFLE.

MRS. E. C. STARIN.

One cup of flour, one pint of milk, one spoonful of sugar, and a lump of butter the size of a walnut. Scald the milk, flour and butter together. After the batter is cold stir in the yolks of five eggs. Stir in the whites of the eggs, well beaten, just before baking. Bake in a quick oven; eat with sauce. This is a splendid pudding.

BREAD DEPARTMENT.

———:o:———

YEAST BREAD.

MRS. S. H. LA FETRA.

Boil and mash very fine two or three medium-sized potatoes; add one quart of water, one-half tablespoonful of salt, the same of sugar, and four spoonfuls of best home-made yeast; stir in sufficient flour to make a moderately stiff batter; cover closely, and let it stand over night. In the morning stir down and let it rise again. Then add a pint of warm water and a lump of nice sweet lard; mix in flour and knead well; let rise; mold into pans, and when light, bake in a moderate oven. It is sometimes necessary in warm weather to add a small quantity of soda to the sponge before mixing the bread.

———:o:———

POTATO YEAST.

MRS. S. H. LA FETRA.

Boil and mash very fine two medium-sized potatoes; add one teaspoonful of salt, one tablespoonful of sugar, and one-half teaspoonful of ground ginger; thin with water. When milk-warm, put in one-half lupulin yeast gem, well soaked in warm water. Make fresh every two weeks.

———:o:———

WHITE BREAD.

MRS. J. M. CAMPBELL.

One quart of warm water and one cup of yeast; mix flour enough to make a thick batter; set to rise one hour; mix and knead with more flour, until it is perfectly smooth and will not stick to the hands. Cover with a thick cloth and tin cover over that. Set to rise again in a warm place. When sufficiently raised knead again, using very little flour. Put it in your tins to rise again. Bake in a moderately hot oven. Use the potato yeast. Sift the flour. Use no salt in the bread if potato yeast is used.

————:o:————

CORN BREAD.

MISS M. MCLELLAN.

One cup of corn meal, one cup of flour, and two teaspoonfuls of baking-powder, well mixed; add one cup of milk, one or two beaten eggs, one tablespoonful of sugar, and one teaspoonful of salt.

————:o:————

GRAHAM BREAD.

MRS. J. M. CAMPBELL.

One pint of warm water, half cup of potato yeast, half cup of syrup, half teaspoonful of soda, and enough Graham flour to make a stiff batter. Put in the tin you intend to bake it in; set in a warm place to rise. When sufficiently raised, bake in a moderately hot oven.

————:o:————

MILK YEAST, OR SALT RISING BREAD.

MRS. C. C. LAMB.

One pint wheat midlings; stir into it one tablespoonful of white sugar, one tablespoonful of ginger, one teaspoonful of salt, one teaspoonful of soda. Put the mixture into something tight. The day before you wish to make your bread, take two large tablespoonfuls of this dry mixture, put in a cup and pour boiling water upon it; make it about as thick as yeast, and set it where it will keep warm. Do this at noon, and by night it will be light, though it will not rise high. The next morning take a cup of new milk, and one of boiling water, and a little salt, stir in flour until it is about as thick as for fritters, then add the yeast made the day before (do not be afraid to use it if it is dark, it will not discolor your bread). Set in a kettle of water as hot as you can bear your hand in, and in two or three hours it will be up and foaming; then mix your bread, put it in your pans, let it rise until light, and it is ready to bake.

————:o:————

YEAST.

LOUISE J.

Four large potatoes, three pints boiling water, two handful hops, two tablespoonfuls salt, two tablespoonfuls sugar, one small cup of flour. Pare potatoes and put in boiling water, cover and boil until they break apart; take out and mash fine; leaving water boiling, in which place hops for one minute, then strain and pour over the mashed potatoes; when *almost cold*, add salt, sugar, with flour sprinkled on top; when *cold*, add four big spoonfuls of yeast.

————:o:————

POTATO YEAST.

MRS. J. M. CAMPBELL.

Three large potatoes, pared and cut into small pieces, covered with water, and boiled until quite soft. Mash in the water; add two tablespoons of hops, boiled in half a pint of water and strained. When this cools, add a little of your old yeast. Set to rise.

————:o:————

WHITE BREAD.

MRS. DR. HAZLETINE.

Put into your bread-pan a quantity of flour; in the center of it put a heaping teaspoonful of white sugar, a small half-teaspoonful of salt, piece of lard as large as a walnut, two or more large spoonfuls potato yeast. With a spoon work the lard, yeast, sugar and salt together. Take one cup new milk, pour upon it one cup boiling water; let it cool, and put in your flour. Mix stiff enough to mold, half an hour or more, as you have time, set to rise in a warm place. When raised, cut it and mold into loaves. This quantity makes one good loaf.

————:o:-————

BUNS.

MRS. C. C. LAMB.

Mix a sponge the same as for bread, then add a piece of butter as large as an egg, one and one-half cups sugar, two eggs, one cup of milk, one teaspoonful of soda. Let it rise, put in your tins, and let rise again. Take the white of an egg, beat with sugar, and put on the top as soon as it comes from the oven.

————:o:————

BREAD.

LOUISE J.

Six quarts flour make eight loves; two tablespoonfuls salt, one tablespoonful sugar, one pint yeast, two spoonfuls butter. Mix with a pint of milk, and same of tepid water. Large loaves bake one hour.

————:o:————-

POTATO YEAST.

MRS. DR. HAZELTINE.

Pour upon one cup of grated potato one quart of boiling water; let it stand on the stove and boil for a few minutes, then put in two-thirds of a cup of white sugar, two large spoonfuls of salt; beat it until dissolved, let it cool, and put in potato yeast to raise. It will keep two weeks in a cool place.

————:o:————

CREAM BISCUIT.

MRS. J. M. STEWART.

To one quart of sifted flour add two heaping teaspoonfuls of Dr. Price's cream baking-powder and one coffeecupful of sour cream, into which stir a scant quarter of a teaspoon of soda and a little salt. Use sweet milk enough to mix up the flour so it will roll out easily. Have the oven hot, and bake as quick as possible.

The above makes a superior crust for strawberry short-cake. Roll out the dough in two equal parts; spread a very little butter between them, and when baked they divide easily.

————:o:————

MUFFINS.

MRS. S. B. CASWELL.

One cup of milk, two cups of flour, one teaspoonful of butter, one egg, half teaspoon of soda, one teaspoonful of cream of tartar, and sugar if you like.

————:o:————

CORN BREAD.

MRS. BARROWS.

One cupful of flour, two cupfuls of corn meal, two tablespoonfuls of sugar, two teaspoonfuls of cream of tartar, one teaspoonful of soda, two and a half cupfuls of milk, and three eggs. Beat the yolks and whites separately, and put in last.

————:o:————

STEAMED BROWN BREAD.

MRS. C. C. LAMB.

One cup of sour milk, one teaspoonful of soda, one cup of sweet milk, three-fourths of a cup of syrup, a little salt, one cup of rye flour, one and one-half cups of corn meal, one and one-half cups of Graham flour, and a piece of butter the size of an egg. Should the mixture prove to be too stiff, add a little more sweet milk.

————:o:————

GEMS, FOR BREAKFAST.

MRS. S. B. CASWELL.

One cup of milk, one cup of water, three cups of sifted flour, and a pinch of salt. Beat together ten minutes; pour the mixture into hot buttered pans; bake in a quick oven ten minutes.

———:o:———

MUFFINS.

MRS. C. H. BRADLEY.

One quart of flour, three teaspoonfuls of yeast powder, three eggs, well beaten, two tablespoonfuls of melted butter and one pint of milk. Bake in muffin rings in a quick oven.

———:o:———

ROLLS.

MRS. R. M. WIDNEY.

One egg, one pint of sweet milk, half cup of fresh lard, fourth cup of white sugar, and one heaping tablespoonful of brewers' yeast, which has been soaked in cold water to extract the bitterness of the beer. To the milk add lard, egg, sugar, and salt. Stir in sifted flour enough to make a thin batter; then add the yeast, and let it stand until very light. Mix and knead twenty or thirty minutes; let rise, and roll out. Cut with biscuit cutter, kneading as little as possible. When light again, bake twenty-five minutes.

———:o:———

CORN MEAL CAKES.

MRS. S. B. CASWELL.

One good pint of corn meal, a little salt, a large spoonful of syrup, and a half spoonful of soda. Scald well; then add a handful of flour and one egg. Have plenty of hot fat in a pan, and drop in a spoonful of the batter at a time. Fry quickly.

———:o:———

ROLLS, OR FLUM-DOODLES.

ANONYMOUS.

One pint of potato yeast, one pint of fresh milk; make a sponge and let it rise light; add three eggs, one cup of sugar, one-fourth pound of butter, and a little salt. Make into a soft dough, mixing with a spoon; do not use the hands. Let it get very light; then pinch off small bits; roll out thin; spread lightly with butter, and roll up. Put it into pans, let rise, and bake light brown. The secret is in the manner of preparing, but it is a great success when well done.

———:o:———

SALLY LUNN.

MRS. GEN. STONEMAN.

Rub a piece of butter the size of an egg into a quart of flour; add one tumbler of milk, two eggs, three tablespoonfuls of sugar, two tablespoonfuls of cream of tartar, one teaspoonful of soda, and half a teaspoonful of salt. To be eaten warm, with butter.

———:o:———

BUCKWHEAT BREAD.

MRS. M. G. MOORE.

Two coffee cupfuls of new buttermilk, one egg, well beaten, two tablespoonfuls of rich cream, two tablespoonfuls of molasses, a little salt, one teaspoonful of salaratus, and buckwheat enough to thicken the same as for corn bread. Bake one-half hour.

———:o:———

BROWN BREAD.

MRS. JENNIE STAFFORD, SANTA ANA.

Three cupfuls of sour milk, one teaspoonful of soda, one cupful of syrup, two cupfuls of corn meal, two cupfuls of Graham flour, and one cupful of wheat flour. Steam two and a half hours.

———:o:———

MARYLAND BISCUITS.

ANONYMOUS.

One quart of the best flour, a bit of lard (fresh) the size of an egg, a little salt, a quarter of a teaspoonful of cream of tartar, thoroughly mixed with the flour. Make a stiff dough by mixing with ice-water; knead until soft; mold by hand, and bake immediately in a moderately hot oven.

———:o:———

BOSTON BROWN BREAD.

MARY A. LINDLEY.

Take three cupfuls of sour milk and one of molasses, three cupfuls of Graham flour and one of corn meal. Add one heaping teaspoonful of soda, and beat well together. Steam three hours.

———:o:———

SQUASH BISCUITS.

MISS MARY MCLELLAN.

Two cups of sifted squash, one tablespoonful of butter, one of lard, two large spoonfuls of sugar, two cups of milk, flour enough to roll out, and one cup of yeast. Boil the milk, sugar, butter, and lard together; let it cool, and mix with the squash, flour, and yeast. Let it rise over night, and make into biscuit in the morning.

———:o:———

BROWN BREAD.

MRS. DR. HAZLETON.

Two cups of sour milk, two large spoonfuls of molasses, and one teaspoonful of soda, dissolved in half cup of water. Stir in an equal quantity of corn and Graham meal until it makes a stiff batter; put it in a two-quart tapering pail; cover tight, and boil in a kettle of water an hour; then take out, take off the cover, and bake slowly one hour.

———:o:———

TEA BISCUITS—ENGLISH.

ANONYMOUS.

Four tumblers of sifted flour, one-fourth pound of good butter, one teaspoonful of soda, two of cream of tartar, one dessert-spoonful of baking powder, and one and a half tumblers of milk. . Mix the butter, cream of tartar, and baking powder well into the flour; then add the milk, with the soda dissolved in it, and mix quickly with a spoon. Knead well on a board; roll an inch thick, and cut with a sharp cutter. Bake twenty or twenty-five minutes in a quick oven.

————:o:————

CREAM OF TARTAR BISCUITS.

MRS. MILLIKEN.

One quart of flour, three heaping teaspoonfuls of pure cream of tartar, a piece of butter two-thirds the size of an egg, well worked in flour, one heaping teaspoonful of Babbit's salaratus, dissolved in sweet milk. Make the dough as soft as can be kneaded conveniently; roll a half inch thick, cut in biscuits, and bake in a quick oven.

————:o:————

STRAWBERRY SHORT-CAKE.

MISS MARY MCLELLAN.

One quart of flour, sifted dry, with two large teaspoonfuls of baking powder, a little salt, and one tablespoonful of white sugar. Add three tablespoonfuls of butter, and milk enough to form a soft dough. Bake in a round tin, and when partially cooled, split, spread with butter, and cover with a layer of strawberries, well sprinkled with white sugar. Lay the other half on top, and spread in the same way.

————:o:————

PARKER HOUSE ROLLS.

MRS. L. S. E. LONGSTREET.

Two quarts of flour, two tablespoonfuls of butter, one teaspoonful of salt, and half teacupful of sugar; mix well through the flour with your hands; make a hole in the middle of the flour and pour in a pint of scalded milk; after it cools put in a small cup of yeast, and set to rise at nine o'clock. About noon stir it well with a spoon; let rise again, and at four roll them out a quarter of an inch thick; cut round and fold over like an envelope, with a small piece of butter between; let rise again for an hour, and bake in a quick oven.

———:o:———

CORN MEAL PANCAKES.

L. C. GOODWIN.

One pint of sour milk, a teaspoonful of soda, one cupful of flour and one of meal, a little salt, and two eggs, white and yolks well beaten separately, and whites added last.

———:o:———

RICE CAKES.

MISS MARY MCLELLAN.

To one teacupful of cold boiled rice put one and one-half cupfuls of flour, two eggs, one tablespoonful of cornstarch, one teaspoonful of salt, two tablespoonfuls of sugar, and sour milk enough to make a batter. Mix smoothly, and add one teaspoonful of soda and a little melted butter. Cook as griddle cakes.

———:o:———

SARATOGA ROLLS.

MRS. GEORGE CLARK.

One quart of water, two ounces of butter, one teacupful of home-made yeast, and a little salt. Mix in the evening, as thick as you can stir with a spoon; put it in a warm place. Just before going to bed, knead it up, and cover till morning. An hour before breakfast make it into small buns, put them in pans, and let stand until light. Bake fifteen or twenty minutes in a hot oven.

———:o:———

MRS. SMITH'S HOT MUFFINS.

MRS. I. S. MAYO.

One quart of warm milk, two eggs, well beaten, a piece of butter the size of an egg, one teacupful of yeast, a little salt, and enough flour to make a batter as thick as for pan-

cakes. Let it rise till morning; then add a small teaspoonful of soda, dissolved in a little hot water. Have your gem-
irons quite hot, and put a spoonful in each. Bake. in a
quick oven. Splendid!

————:o:————

GRAHAM GEMS.

MISS MARY MCLELLAN.

One and a half pints of Graham flour and three teaspoonfuls of baking-powder, well mixed. Rub in one tablespoonful of butter; add salt, one beaten egg, and one tablespoonful of sugar. Stir all to a batter with sweet milk;
drop into hot gem-pans and bake in a quick oven.

————:o:————

POTATO PANCAKES.

MRS. H. K. S. O'MELVENY.

Grate some raw potatoes; let the water drain off a little; then add three well-beaten eggs to a pint of potatoes,
some salt, and a spoonful of flour. Fry slowly in hot lard.

————:o:————

MAG. MADDIN'S INDIAN CAKE.

MRS. I. S. MAYO.

Two cupfuls of flour, one cupful of corn meal, one egg,
two tablespoonfuls of sugar, and half a teaspoonful of salt;
stir up with sour milk, in which has been dissolved a teaspoonful of soda. Make a thin batter, and bake in a sheet.

————:o:————

MUFFINS.

MRS. S. C. HUBBELL.

Two eggs, a pint of flour, one teacupful of milk or
cream, a piece of butter half the size of an egg, a little salt,
a heaping tablespoonful of sugar, and one teaspoonful of
baking powder. Mix the baking powder and salt in the
flour. Beat the eggs; add to the yolks, first, the milk and

sugar, then the butter (melted), then the flour, and then the whites. Beat well after it is all mixed, and bake in a hot oven.

————:o:————

CORN BREAD.

MRS. MARY BACKMAN.

One pint of sifted corn meal, half cup of sifted flour, one tablespoonful of lard, rubbed into the flour, half cup of milk, one egg, one teaspoonful of salt, and one teaspoonful of baking powder.

————:o:————

MUFFINS.

MISS MARY MCLELLAN.

Two and a half cupfuls of flour, a piece of butter the size of an egg, one tablespoonful of sugar, two eggs, salt, one and a half cupfuls of milk, and one cupful of yeast. Let it stand to rise over night, and do not stir in the morning, but dip out into muffin rings or gem pans.

————:o:————

MARYLAND BISCUIT.

MRS. M. E. J.

One quart of flour, a teaspoonful of salt, one table-spoonful of lard, and a half pint of lukewarm water. Make the dough very stiff, working the lard and salt in thoroughly before the water is added. Beat or knead till the dough is soft, and blisters. Prick each biscuit with a fork before baking.

————:o:————

CORN CRUST.

MRS. I. S. MAYO.

One pint of corn meal, one pint of boiling water, one tablespoonful of sugar, half teaspoonful of salt, and one egg. Pour the boiling water on the meal, sugar, and salt; mix well, stir in the beaten egg, spread thin in a dripping-pan, smooth over with a knife, dipped in cold water, and score it. Bake in a quick oven.

————:o:————

RICE WAFFLES.

MRS. M. E. J.

One and a half cupfuls of boiled rice and two cupfuls of flour. Add salt, and mix with milk to a thick batter. Beat separately two eggs, and add last.

————:o:————

SQUASH BREAKFAST CAKE.

MRS. I. S. MAYO.

One pint of sifted squash, one egg, a small cup of sugar, a piece of butter the size of an egg, two tablespoonfuls of yeast, and enough flour to mold up. Set to rise over night. In the morning dissolve a teaspoonful of soda in a little water and put into the mixture; mold, and cut into biscuit. Let them rise, and bake fifteen minutes.

————:o:————

YEAST–POWDER BISCUIT.

MRS. L. M. THOMPSON.

Mix well with one quart of flour one teaspoonful of yeast-powder and a little salt; add a small piece of butter or lard and a cupful of sweet milk, stirred in with a spoon. Work the dough as little as possible; roll out, and bake in a quick oven.

————:o:————

FRENCH ROLLS.

MRS. M. E. J.

Sift a pound of flour; rub in two ounces of butter and a little salt; mix in the beaten whites of three eggs and a tablespoonful of strong yeast; add enough milk for a stiff dough; cover and set before the fire to rise. Put it on a bread board, divide it into rolls, lay in a floured pan, and bake in a quick oven about ten minutes.

————:o:————

CORN BREAD.

MRS. H. K. S. O'MELVENY.

Turn one pint of boiling water or milk on as much corn meal; when lukewarm, add one spoonful of lard or butter, one of sugar, two eggs, well beaten, three tablespoonfuls of flour, and one teaspoonful of baking powder. If too stiff, add a little cold milk.

————:o:————

CORN BUNS.

MRS. GEN. STONEMAN.

One quart of milk, three eggs, and a small piece of butter. Stir in meal for a batter just thick enough to drop from a spoon. Bake in a hot oven.

————:o:————

FLAP–JACKS.

MRS. T. S. STANWAY.

Take two pounds of wheat flour and a teaspoonful of salt; make a pretty thick batter with warm water; add two good tablespoonfuls of brewers' yeast. Set to rise over night; bake the same as buckwheat cakes. Very nice.

————:o:————

FRENCH ROLLS.

MRS. GEN. STONEMAN.

One pint of warm water, two tablespoonfuls of white sugar, one-half cupful of lard, and two-thirds of a cupful of hop-potato yeast. First put the lard into the warm water; then add the salt, sugar, and yeast. Knead up hard with flour, and put to rise. The next morning knead it an hour, or chop with a chopping-knife instead of an hour's kneading. Cut out with a large-sized biscuit-cutter; wet the top of each biscuit with a little melted butter, and turn over on one side. Do not put them close together. You can bake what you need and set the rest away; it will keep a long time.

————:o:————

MUFFINS.

MRS. DR. FRENCH.

Warm a quart of milk, and melt in it a quarter of a pound of the best butter, cut into bits. Beat four eggs until very light, and stir into the milk. When quite cold, by degrees stir in enough sifted flour to make a batter as thick as you can well stir. Add at least three tablespoonfuls of bakers' yeast. Set to rise in a warm place. Bake in muffin rings.

————:o:————

PHILADELPHIA MUFFINS.

RELIABLE.

One quart of milk, three eggs, one-fourth pound of lard, the same of butter, and a little salt. Put the butter, lard, and salt in the milk, stand it on the range, and let it get just warm; then stir in enough sifted flour to make a stiff batter. Beat it well; then put in a small teacupful of yeast, and set it to rise. If you want them for tea, set them to rise about an hour. Use tin rings. Do not fill them quite full. They require but a few moments to bake. The milk must be only lukewarm.

————:o:————

BREAD.

MRS. R. N. C. WILSON.

Boil three potatoes; mash them well; add a teaspoonful of salt and two of sugar; also enough boiling water to make rather a thin batter. Let it cool, and when lukewarm, add one Price's yeast cake, soaked in a little water. One cake is sufficient for four loaves of bread. Add two and a half cups of flour. Let this rise until light; then stir in enough flour to make a sponge. Let it remain in a warm place until morning, when it should be kneaded at least twenty minutes. Return the dough to the pan, and when light, separate it into four loaves and let it rise again. When light, let it bake an hour.

————:o:———— —

SPANISH WAFERS.

MRS. T. S. STANWAY.

Take three eggs; mix them with as much flour as will permit it to be rolled out as thin as possible. Cut it in squares with a jaging iron, and fry in hot lard. Lay them on a hot dish and throw sugar and cinnamon over, if liked.

————:o:————

POCKET–BOOKS—BREAD.

MRS. F. D. BOVARD.

One quart of new milk, one cupful of yeast, one teaspoonful of salt, and one tablespoonful of butter. When light, knead and roll out, and cut into small, oblong pieces. Spread one-half of each piece with a mixture of butter and sugar, and fold together; then lay them in a baking pan to raise.

————:o:————

CORN CAKES.

MRS. T. S. STANWAY.

One cup of sweet milk, a tablespoonful of white sugar, one egg, two tablespoonfuls of butter, one teaspoonful of soda, and two of cream of tartar. Make as stiff as batter. They are delicious for breakfast.

————:o:————

A NICE DISH FOR BREAKFAST.

MRS. T. S. STANWAY.

Take some slices of bread, cutting off the crust; make a batter of three eggs and a pint of milk; soak the bread in it. Put some butter in a frying-pan, and fry the slices of bread to a nice brown.

University of Southern California.

:o:

THE FIRST BUILDING IS NOW COMPLETED, AND THE Literary College opened its first term October 6th, 1880, with the following Departments :

1. Preparatory, *2. Elective.*
3. Normal, *4. Scientific.*
5. Classical.

The building is new, commodious, and pleasantly situated, on the University Grounds. Sufficient apparatus has been secured for the different Departments.

Good arrangements will be made for Boarding.

FACULTY.

Rev. M. M. Bovard, A. M., President, and Professor of Moral, Mental and Natural Sciences.
Rev. F. D. Bovard, A. M., Prof. Ancient Languages and Mathematics
J. P. Widney, A. M, M. D., Prof. of English Literature, Physiology and Hygiene.
Mrs. Jennie Allen Bovard, M. S., Professor of English Language and History.
Mrs. Annie S. Averill, M. S., Teacher in Mathematics and Normal Instruction.
Rev. G. H. Bollinger,   -   -   -   -   Teacher in German
Miss Josephine T. Clarke, Teacher in French & Instrumental Music
Madame Marra,   -   -   -   -   Teacher in Vocal Music
Miss Maria Pruneda,   -   -   -   -   Teacher in Spanish
Mrs. C. P. Bradfield,   -   -   -   -   Teacher in Drawing

CALENDAR FOR 1880-81.

First Term Begins,	Sept. 15,	Second Term Ends,	March 31,
First Term Ends,	Dec. 23,	Third Term Begins,	April 4,
Second Term Begins,	Jan. 4,	Third Term Ends,	June 24.

TERMS OF ADMISSION.

Students entering the Freshman Class must pass examination upon the Studies in the Preparatory Course, and be over fourteen years of age.

For further information send for circular, or apply to

M. M. BOVARD, A. M., PRESIDENT,

Los Angeles, Cal.

PUDDING DEPARTMENT.

CHRISTMAS PUDDING.

MRS. H. C. AUSTIN.

One pound of raisins, seeded and cut fine, one pound of currants, thoroughly washed, one pound of leaf suet, freed from strings and chopped fine, one pint of bread crumbs, half pint of sifted flour, a quarter of a pound of best sugar, one tablespoonful of powdered mace and cinnamon, mixed, and two ground nutmegs. Beat nine eggs, yolks and whites separately, and add one pint of rich milk in turn with the bread crumbs and flour. Mix with the sugar the grated rind and juice of two lemons or oranges. Mix all together, stirring hard, adding the fruit after it has been dredged in flour. Steam six hours in a tin vessel, covered tight, in a kettle of boiling water.

A most excellent sauce for this pudding may be made in the following manner: Two cupfuls of sugar, one cupful of butter, and four eggs. Cream the butter and sugar; beat the yolks and whites of the eggs, and add them. Lastly, add one cup of boiling water. Flavor to taste.

————:o:————

EXCELLENT RICE PUDDING.

MRS. C. G. DU BOIS.

One quart of milk, one-fourth cupful of raw rice; and salt, sugar, and flavor to taste. Add some seeded raisins, and bake two and a half hours in a very moderate oven.

————:o:————

ICED PUDDING.

MRS. J. G. HOWARD.

Make a custard with a pint of milk, two eggs, and six ounces of sugar. Beat the eggs and sugar together, stir the hot milk on them, return to the fire, and stir until they thicken. When cool, flavor with vanilla; freeze, and add a pint of whipped cream, after which stir in six ounces of candied fruit—citron, pears, pineapple, cherries—all cut in very small squares, and a few chopped raisins and currants. Repack, and set away to finish freezing.

————:o:————

PLUM PUDDING.

MISS MARY MCLELLAN.

Soak a loaf of baker's bread in two quarts of milk until well softened. Stir in thoroughly six eggs, a little salt, and a tablespoonful of molasses. Have a deep earthen dish well buttered, and put into it a little of the mixture; then a layer of seeded raisins. Fill the dish with alternate layers of the mixture and the raisins. Bake four or five hours. After it is well browned, keep the oven at a moderate heat. Eat with a rich sauce.

————:o:————

BIBIFAUX.

MRS. E. WORKMAN.

Three pints of cream, beaten to a froth, half pound of white sugar, and six sheets of Cooper's isinglass. To one and one-fourth pints of water add the sugar, isinglass and one-third of a vanilla bean. Let it simmer till thoroughly dissolved; remove and strain. Let cool until it begins to thicken; then pour gently over it the beaten cream, stirring briskly until all is added.

————:o:————

BATTER PUDDING.

MRS. S. B. CASWELL.

Six or eight eggs, one quart of milk, a small bowl of flour and a little salt. Bake quickly.

————:o:————

A DELICIOUS PUDDING.

MRS. ADELIA HALL.

Two cupfuls of bread crumbs, one and a half cupfuls of white sugar, five eggs, one tablespoonful of butter, one quart of fresh milk, and a half cupful of jelly or jam. Rub the butter and one cupful of sugar together; then add the beaten yolks of the eggs; beat all to a cream; then add the bread crumbs, which have previously been soaked in the milk. Bake in a pudding dish (not filling more than two-thirds full) until the custard is set; then draw to the mouth of the oven and spread over the jelly or jam; cover this with a meringue made of the beaten whites of the eggs and half cupful of sugar. Put back in the oven, and allow to remain until the meringue begins to color. To be eaten with cold cream.

———:o:———

PORTLAND PUDDING.

MISS MARY MCLELLAN.

Three-fourths of a cupful of rice, cooked thoroughly in one quart of milk. Then stir into it the yolks of four eggs, a small piece of butter, the grated peel of one lemon, and three tablespoonfuls of sugar, all well beaten together. Put it in a dish and cover with a meringue composed of the whites of four eggs, four tablespoonfuls of sugar, and the juice of a lemon. Brown delicately in the oven.

———:o:———

SYBILS' PUDDING.

MRS. S. B. CASWELL.

One big bowl of grated bread, one bowl of sugar, one bowl of chopped suet, one bowl of currants, and nine eggs. Cook six hours.

———:o:———

BATTER PUDDING.

RELIABLE.

One pint of milk, three eggs, four tablespoonfuls of sifted flour, and one salt-spoonful of salt. Break the eggs into the flour and beat well together. Bake twenty minutes.

———:o:———

APPLE PUDDING.

MISS MARY MCLELLAN.

One pint of flour, one teaspoonful of baking-powder, one of salt, one tablespoonful of butter and water enough to make a soft dough. Fill a pudding dish with apples, pared, cored, and quartered; add a little water, and cover with the dough. Put the pudding on top of the stove and cover tightly with another pan. Cook one hour. Serve with sauce.

---:o:---

SUET PUDDING.

MRS. J. M. STEWART.

One cupful of syrup or half cupful of brown sugar, one cupful of milk, two-thirds of a cupful of suet, one cupful of raisins, one teaspoonful of soda, and flour enough to make a stiff batter. Boil steadily three hours.

---:o:---

LEMON PUDDING.

RELIABLE.

One lemon, two ounces of butter, two ounces of sugar, four eggs, a large tablespoonful of corn-starch, and one pint of boiling milk. Beat the yolks well; add the sugar, butter, grated peel and juice of the lemon. Pour the boiling milk in last. Bake in a well buttered dish till set, or for half an hour. Whisk the whites of the eggs to a solid froth, adding a little sugar, and drop in spoonfuls over the top when the pudding is cold. Put in the oven for two or three minutes, to set.

---:o:---

CHRISTMAS PUDDING.

MRS. FLANDERS.

One pound of bread crumbs, one pound of currants, one pound of raisins (seeded), one pound of suet, a quarter of a pound of citron, chopped fine, one cup of molasses, eleven eggs, two teaspoonfuls of yeast-powder, and all kinds of spices. Boil five hours in a cloth.

Sauce: Two cups of sugar, one cup of butter, and five eggs. Beat the sugar, butter and yolks of the eggs to a cream; froth the whites of the eggs and beat in; then pour in a cup of boiling water.

---:o:---

DOG IN THE BLANKET.

MRS. M. E. J.

Slice bread a fourth of an inch thick, cut off the crust, butter it, and lay it in a pudding dish; cut some slices small, to fit your dish smoothly. Place a layer of bread and one of jam alternately, until the dish is filled, jam on top. Make a custard of three eggs and a pint and a half of milk, with about three tablespoonfuls of sugar; pour it over the pudding and let it stand half an hour. Bake thirty minutes. Serve with hard sauce, colored with the juice of the jam, such as you have used in the pudding.

---:o:---

SWEET APPLE PUDDING.

RELIABLE.

Take one cupful of sweet milk, one teaspoonful of salt, two tablespoonfuls of sugar, and two eggs, well beaten; mix with sufficient flour to make as stiff as for dumplings; then stir in two quarts of chopped apples until thoroughly mixed with the dough. Put into a pan greased with butter, and bake one hour and a half. To be eaten either hot or cold, with butter and sugar. Season to taste.

---:o:---

CHEESE PUDDING.

LOUISE J.

Four eggs, one cupful of sugar, half a small cupful of grated Parmesan cheese, one cupful of flour, two teaspoonfuls of yeast-powder, one pinch of salt, and one quart of milk. Bake half an hour; serve as soon as baked, and eat with hard sauce.

---:o:---

STEAM PUDDING.

MRS. PARCELS.

One coffee-cupful of sour milk, one coffee-cupful of molasses, half coffee-cupful of butter, four coffee-cupfuls of flour, one teaspoonful of soda, one teaspoonful of cinnamon, half teaspoonful of cloves, and one cupful of raisins. Steam three hours.

---:o:---

PLUM PUDDING.

MRS. H. MCLELLAN.

Remove the top crust from a fresh loaf of baker's bread; break in pieces, and pour over it one quart of sweet milk. Let it soak a few hours; then add six eggs, a small cupful of sugar, one pound of seeded raisins, salt, and a little cinnamon. Bake five or six hours. Pour a little milk on the pudding when baking, to prevent its being too stiff.

———:o:———

SALEM PUDDING.

MRS. C. G. DU BOIS.

One cupful of suet, chopped fine, one cupful of molasses, one cupful of sweet milk, three and a half cupfuls of flour, one cupful of raisins, a little salt, one tablespoonful of cloves, and three teaspoonfuls of yeast-powder. Steam three hours.

———:o:———

LEMON CHEESE–CAKES.

RELIABLE.

A quarter of a pound of butter, three-fourths of a pound of lump sugar, powdered, six eggs, well beaten, the grated rind of two lemons, and the juice of three lemons. Cook in a brass or enameled pan till the sugar is dissolved and the mixture becomes of the thickness of honey.

———:o:———

COTTAGE PUDDING.

MRS. C. G. DU BOIS.

One cup of sugar, one cup of sweet milk, a third of a cup of melted butter, one egg, two small teaspoonfuls of cream of tartar, one teaspoonful of soda, and one pint of sifted flour. Bake three-quarters of an hour. To be eaten with sauce.

———:o:———

QUEEN OF PLUM PUDDINGS.

MRS. HAMILTON.

One pound of butter, one pound of suet, freed from strings and chopped fine, one pound of sugar, two and a half pounds of flour, two pounds of raisins, seeded, chopped and dredged with flour, two pounds of currants, a quarter of a pound of citron, chopped fine, twelve eggs, whites and yolks beaten separately, one pint of milk, one cup of boiled-down cider, half ounce of cloves, half ounce of mace, and two grated nutmegs. Cream the butter and sugar; beat in the yolks when you have whipped them smooth and light;

next put in the milk, then the flour, alternately with the beaten whites, the cider and spices, and lastly the fruit, well dredged with flour. Mix all thoroughly; wring out your pudding cloth in hot water; flour well inside, pour in the mixture, and boil five hours.

———:o:———

QUICK BAKED PUDDING.

MRS. C. G. DU BOIS.

Five tablespoonfuls of flour, five well-beaten eggs, salt, five tablespoonfuls of cold milk. Mix well, and turn into one quart of boiling milk. Bake fifteen or twenty minutes. Eat with sauce.

———:o:———

DANDY PUDDING.

MRS. BARROWS.

One quart of milk, boiled in water. Mix two spoonfuls of corn-starch with the yolks of four eggs and half cup of sugar; pour into the boiling milk; stir quickly, and take off at once. Beat the whites of the eggs with half cup of sugar, and spread over the pudding when cool. Put it in the oven and brown. Flavor with essence of lemon. To be eaten cold.

———:o:———

BAKED APPLE DUMPLINGS.

MRS. C. G. DU BOIS.

Take a half pint of raised dough, work into it a large spoonful of shortening, roll out, fold it, and set aside to lighten. When well raised, divide it into six parts and roll them out thin. Have ready six good-sized, tart apples, cored, and the holes filled with sugar and butter; close the dough neatly over the apples, and turn the folded side down in a deep dish. Let them stand till light; then sprinkle sugar, small pieces of butter, and any spice you like, betwen the apples. Pour one teacupful of water over them, and bake three-fourths of an hour.

———:o:———

ORANGE PUDDING.

MRS. M. E. J.

Enough oranges for four cups of juice, which must be put on to boil. Grate the peel of four oranges and squeeze the juice into a baking dish; add to this one and a half cups of sugar, the yolks of four eggs, well beaten, one teaspoonful of butter, eight tablespoonfuls of corn-starch, mixed in a little cold water or orange juice. Stir all well together, and set the pudding dish on the stove to warm. Add the boiling juice, and stir (with the dish still on the stove) until it is thickened. Bake about half an hour. Make a meringue of the four whites, well thickened with powdered sugar, and put on top of the pudding, returning it to the oven long enough to make it a very light brown.

——————:o:——————

TAPIOCA PUDDING.

MRS. C. G. DU BOIS.

Three coffee-cupfuls of tapioca, and nine coffee-cupfuls of water (cold). Let it soak one night. Add the rind of two lemons and the juice of one, two coffee-cupfuls of sugar, and soft, tart apples. Pour the tapioca over the apples and bake. Cream sauce.

——————:o:——————

FOAM PUDDING.

MRS. M. G. MOORE.

One teaspoonful of boiled rice, salted, three eggs, one cupful sugar. Spread the rice in the pudding-pan; grate a little nutmeg over it; beat the whites of the eggs stiff, and spread over the rice, then beat the yolks and sugar together and spread on top. Bake twenty minutes in a moderate oven.

——————:o:——————

BOILED BATTER PUDDING.

SAN GABRIEL.

Three tablespoonfuls of flour, three eggs, whites and yolks beaten separately, and milk enough to make it like a thin cream. Boil one hour. Take it up as soon as done. Serve with wine sauce.

——————:o:——————

PLAIN BATTER PUDDING.

MRS. COL. GEORGE SMITH.

Six eggs, three tablespoonfuls of sifted flour (the spoons must be heaped), and two cupfuls milk. Beat the eggs separately, and very light; mix the milk and flour, then add the yolks, lastly the whites; after which, bake immediately in a moderately hot oven. Serve hot, and eat with stirred butter and sugar sauce.

————:o:————

APPLE SAGO PUDDING.

MRS. C. G. DU BOIS.

One cupful of sago in six cupfuls of water; put near the stove to swell. In the meantime stew ten or twelve tart apples; mix with the swelled sago, and bake three-quarters of an hour. Eat with cream and sugar.

————:o:————

BAKED APPLE DUMPLING.

MRS. M. G. MOORE.

Take one-half pint raised dough, work into it a large spoonful of shortening; roll out, fold it, and set aside to lighten. When well raised, cut into six pieces, roll out thin; have ready six good sized apples, pared and cored, the holes filled with sugar and butter. Close the dough neatly over the apples, and turn that side down in a deep dish. Let it stand one hour to lighten, then sprinkle sugar, spice (any kind you prefer), and small pieces of butter, over and between the apples, and pour over all a teacupful of water. Bake an hour.

————:o:————

SAUCE FOR PUDDINGS.

MRS. M. E. HOYT.

One large cupful of sugar and half cupful of butter, beat together till light. Break into the mixture the yolk of one egg and the whites of two, and beat well. Flavor to taste, and place on the fire. Stir until it smokes, but do not let it boil.

————:o:————

SNOW PUDDING.

MRS. E. C. STARIN.

One box of gelatine, cover with cold water and let soak half an hour; add a pint of boiling water, stir until dissolved, set away to cool. When cool, add the whites of four eggs beaten to solid froth, with the juice of two lemons, and two cups of sugar; beat all well together, and let stand until a stiff jelly. For a sauce, take yolks of the four eggs, and a pint of boiling milk, sweetened and flavored to taste; boil to a custard.

————:o:————

LEMON PUDDING.

MRS. C. G. DU BOIS.

Half pound of fine bread crumbs, a quarter of a pound of well-chopped suet, a quarter of a pound of sifted sugar, the rind of two lemons and the juice of one, or the juice of three lemons (juice must be first strained), two eggs, thoroughly beaten, and a little salt. Mix all well together and steam one hour. Eat with sauce.

————:o:————

STEAMED PUDDING.

MRS. L. CREEK.

One cupful of sugar, one cupful of milk, one-half cupful of currants, five cupfuls of flour, two eggs, well beaten, and two teaspoonfuls of baking powder. Steam an hour and a half.

————:o:————

CORN MEAL PUDDING.

MRS. S. YARNELL.

One cupful of corn meal, stirred in one quart of boiling milk, one cupful of molasses, half cupful of chopped suet, one chopped apple, and a pinch of salt. Put in a buttered pudding dish and sprinkle with cinnamon. Pour over a pint of cold milk. Do not stir the pudding. Bake slowly three hours. To be eaten with a sweet sauce.

————:o:————

KATY–DID PUDDING.

MRS. M. G. MOORE.

One quart of boiling water, three tablespoonfuls of corn-starch (wet in a little cold water), a pinch of salt, and the whites of three eggs. Stir the corn-starch into the boiling water, and let boil about four minutes, then stir into it the stiff whites—do not let the eggs boil. Turn into molds until cold, then pour over it the following cold custard: One quart boiling milk, yolks of three eggs, one tablespoonful of corn-starch (wet in a little cold milk), sugar and salt to taste. Let the milk boil, stir into it the wet starch, eggs and sugar; as it cools, flavor with lemon.

———:o:———

BLACK PUDDING.

MRS. E. C. STARIN.

One cupful suet, one cupful molasses, one cupful milk (sweet), three and a half cupfuls flour, one cupful fruit, one teaspoonful soda. Steam two hours.

———:o:———

QUEEN OF PUDDINGS.

MRS. JOHN FOY, SAN BERNARDINO.

Beat together the yolks of four eggs, two tablespoonfuls of melted butter, one cupful of sugar, one quart of milk, and one pint of bread-crumbs; flavor with lemon extract, and bake in a deep dish. When done, spread over the top a layer of tart jelly. Beat the whites of four eggs, add a tablespoonful of powdered sugar, and spread over the jelly. Brown slightly in the oven.

———:o:———

PLAIN PUDDING.

MRS. R. M. WIDNEY.

Three tablespoonfuls of flour, three tablespoonfuls of cold milk, three eggs, and one and a half pints of scalded milk. Bake in the oven, and serve with a sauce of butter and sugar, flavored with vanilla, or any sauce preferred.

———:o:———

COTTAGE PUDDING.

MRS. E. C. STARIN.

One cupful sugar, one cupful milk, one egg, one pint sifted flour, baking powder, two teaspoonfuls.

PIE DEPARTMENT.

————:o:————

LEMON PIE.

MRS. JOHN FOY, SAN BERNARDINO.

One cup of sugar, three eggs, a small lump of butter, a teacupful of milk, and the juice, with the grated yellow part of the rind, of a lemon. Roll the lemon and squeeze the juice over one-half the sugar; beat the yolks and mix together, adding the butter and milk last. Fill the pie and put in the oven. Beat the whites of the eggs with the other half of the sugar, and when the pie has baked, spread it over and brown in the oven.

————:o:————

GERMAN PIE.

MRS. II. K. S. O'MELVENY.

Take a piece of bread dough (if made with milk, all the better), and work in some butter. Cove the bottom of a pie plate or dripping-pan with the dough, and let it raise a short time. Then peel some free-stone peaches (if small), halve them, if large, quarter them), and set them on the dough, the inside uppermost. Fill these with sugar, and bake. Any other fruit may be substituted if desired. This pie can be eaten by any dyspeptic.

———— ~ :o:————

CREAM PIE.

SAN GABRIEL.

One cupful of flour, half cupful of sugar, two eggs, one teaspoonful cream of tartar, and half teaspoonful of soda. Bake in shallow round pans.

Cream for filling: One tablespoonful of cornstarch, one pint of milk (reserving enough to wet the cornstarch), one tablespoonful of sugar, and two eggs, using the whites for frosting.

————:0:————

LEMON TARTS.

MRS. L. CHEEK.

Take two large lemons, grate off the yellow rind, and squeeze out the juice; three large cupfuls of white sugar, six eggs, not separated, and butter the size of an egg. Beat all well together, put in a bowl, and set in boiling water. Let it cook to a thick custard, stirring frequently, and then fill the pastry.

————:0:————

POTATO PIE.

RELIABLE.

Boil eight potatoes the size (when peeled) of an egg; mash fine; add four eggs, one cupful of sugar, and half cupful of butter, a little nutmeg, and one pint of milk. Bake with an under-crust only.

————:0:————

PEACH MERINGUE.

MRS. GEORGE CLARK.

Select a pie-plate that is not too deep, and after arranging a lower crust, fill with peaches, pared, halved, and stoned; sprinkle sugar over them, and bake until done. When cool, spread over it the whites of two eggs, beaten very light; flavor with vanilla. Sprinkle over the top three tablespoonfuls of fine sugar, and brown in the oven for a few minutes.

————:0:————

PUFF PASTE.

MRS. JOHN SMITH.

Two pounds of finely sifted flour, two pounds of butter; put the flour on a marble slab, make a hole in the pile, and add the yolks of four eggs. Work the butter in a napkin until quite free from water; two pinches of salt and juice of half a lemon. Cut up in small pieces one quarter of the butter, and work all this into the paste of eggs and flour, adding as much tepid water as will make the paste smooth.

Beat one-quarter of the remainder of the butter to an inch in thickness; roll out the paste to four times the size; lay the butter on the center of the paste, and cover up on each side; roll ont to three times its original size; repeat twice, putting in a part of the butter each time. Cover for half an hour, when it is ready for use.

————:o:————

LEMON PIE, EXTRA NICE.

MRS. S. SPEEDY.

Four lemons, one cupful water, one cupful sugar, two tablespoonfuls flour, three eggs, two tablespoonfuls sugar. Squeeze out the juice, add the yolks of three eggs, two tablespoonfuls of flour, one cupful sugar; work this mass in a smooth paste, then add a cupful of boiling water; set it in some boil'ng water until it cooks. Bake your crust, then pour in the sauce; beat the whites of three eggs to a stiff froth, adding two tablespoonfuls of sugar; spread this on your pies; set in the oven. Bake a light brown. This quantity is enough for two pies.

————:o:————

GOOD PIE CRUST.

MRS. J. M. CAMPBELL.

One quart flour, one teaspoonful baking powder; put this through a sieve: four tablespoonfuls lard, one teaspoonful salt. Rub all into the flour; mix with one teacupful of water.

————:o:————

PASTRY.

MRS. ADELIA HALL.

A well-beaten egg, rubbed with a piece of cloth over the lower crust of pies will prevent the juice from soaking through it. Puff-paste should be made of sweet, solid butter. The juice of fruit pies, if thickened with a little corn-starch, will not boil over.

————:o:————

CREAM PIES.

MISS MARY MCLELLAN.

Three eggs, one cupful of white sugar, one tablespoonful of water, one and a half teaspoonfuls of baking-powder, and one and a half cupfuls of flour. Bake in two tins. Boil one pint of milk and, stir into it two eggs, one cupful of sugar, and one scant cupful of flour. Let it cook until sufficiently thick; then add a small piece of butter and the grated peel of a fresh lemon. Split the cakes and fill with the cream.

————:o:————

WASHINGTON PIE.

MRS. S. SPEEDY.

Four eggs, one cupful of sugar, one of flour, a lump of butter the size of an egg, one teaspoonful of soda, and two teaspoonfuls of cream of tartar, dissolved in two tablespoonfuls of milk.

The sauce: One large tart apple, pared and grated, the juice of one orange, one cupful of sugar, and one egg. Stir together; set the dish in boiling water long enough to cook the egg; bake, and spread the sauce the same as on jelly cake.

————:o:————

PLAIN LEMON PIE.

MRS. DR. HAZLETINE.

While your pie-crust shells are baking prepare the following filling: Grate the yellow rind of one lemon and squeeze out the juice; put in one cupful of sugar and the yolk of one egg, and stir well together. Upon this pour a large cupful of cold water, into which has been stirred a tablespoonful of corn-starch. Put all in a saucepan, and stir until it is cooked into a clear jelly. The crust being baked, fill them, and from the white of the egg make a meringue to softly cover it. Put in the oven a few minutes, until a delicate brown.

————:o:————

SQUASH PIE.

MRS. R. M. WIDNEY.

One quart of baked squash (Hubbard, if possible), pressed through a sieve, eight eggs, whites and yolks beaten separately, two quarts of milk, two cupfuls of white or very light brown sugar, one teaspoonful of ginger, half teaspoonful of nutmeg, half teaspoonful of cinnamon, and one teaspoonful of salt. Beat all together, and bake in under-crust, without cover. Under-crust first to be rubbed with a well-beaten egg.

———:●:———

APPLE CUSTARD PIE.

MRS. S. SPEEDY.

Pare sour apples and stew until soft, with very little water; then rub them through a colander. Beat three eggs for each pie to be baked, and put in at the rate of one cupful of butter and one of sugar for three pies. Season with nutmeg. A frosting, put upon them as in lemon pie and returned for a few moments to the oven, would at least improve their appearance.

———:o:———

LEMON PIE.

MRS. ADELIA HALL.

Grate the rind of two lemons; beat together the rind, juice, ten tablespoonfuls of loaf sugar, and the yolks of four eggs, until very light; add two tablespoonfuls of water; line a large dish, and fill with the mixture. Bake until the paste is done. Beat the whites stiff, and stir into them two tablespoonfuls [of sugar; spread over the top, and bake a light brown.

———:o:———

CRUST FOR PUMPKIN PIE.

MRS. S. SPEEDY.

Take your pie-dish and butter the tin well; then take some dry corn meal and shake it around in the buttered tin; empty it out, leaving only what sticks to the tin. Have your pumpkin ready, the same as for any pie; pour it in your tin; set it in the oven and bake it. You will be surprised to see what a nice crust it will form.

———:o:———

MINCE-MEAT.

MRS. HAMILTON.

Six pounds of fresh beef, boiled tender, and chopped fine when cold; one pound of beef suet, chopped fine, five pounds of apples, chopped fine, two pounds seeded raisins, two pounds of currants, half pound of citron, two table spoonfuls of cinnamon, one of cloves, one of nutmeg, one of allspice, one of salt, three pounds of brown sugar, three pints of sweet cider, boiled as thick as syrup, and the liquor the meat is boiled in. When you make pies, add a little more apple and boiled-down cider.

————:o:————

LEMON PIE.

MRS. H. C. AUSTIN.

Three-fourths of a cupful of sugar, one tablespoonful of butter, the yolks of three eggs, one tablespoonful of flour in two-thirds of a cupful of water, and half the grated rind and all the juice of one lemon. Beat the whites of the three eggs very light, with a tablespoonful of sugar to each egg, for a meringue to put on the pie when baked. Flavor the meringue with lemon juice; spread it over the pie when baked, and put it back in the oven till it is slightly browned.

————:o:————

LEMON CREAM PIE.

MRS. ADELIA HALL.

The juice and rind of one lemon, one cup of sugar, the yolks of two eggs, three tablespoonfuls sifted flour; milk to fill the plate. Bake until nearly done; take from the oven, pour over it the whites of two eggs, and two tablespoonfuls of powdered sugar, beaten to a stiff froth. Put back in the oven, and brown lightly.

CUSTARDS, CREAMS, FLOATS, SAUCES.

VELVET CREAM.

MRS. H. MCLELLAN.

One-half box of gelatine in one quart of milk, with the yolks of three eggs; place on the stove and stir until it comes to a soft custard. When cold, beat the whites of the eggs to a stiff froth; add six tablespoonfuls of white sugar and one of vanilla flavoring.

———:o:———

CITRON CUSTARD.

MRS. JOHN SMITH.

Six eggs, one cupful of butter, and two cupfuls of granulated sugar. Separate the eggs and beat thoroughly the yolks, and add the whites, which should be whipped to a stiff froth. Wash the butter free from salt, and cream it with the sugar; then add to the eggs; mix thoroughly, and pour into the crust. This will make two custards. Flavor with very little lemon.

———:o:———

STRAWBERRY CUSTARD.

MRS. ANNA OGIER.

Make a nice boiled custard of a quart of milk and five eggs, properly seasoned; boil it till it thickens; take it off the fire and put in the flavoring. Take a gill of sugar and a pint of ripe strawberries; crush them together and pass them through a fine strainer. Take the whites of four of the eggs, and while beating them to a stiff froth, add a gill of sugar, little at a time. Then to the sugar and eggs add the sweetened strawberry juice, beating all the while to make it stiff. This makes a beautiful pink float, which is to be placed on top of the custard. The juice of canned straw-berries may be used.

————:o:————

COFFEE CUSTARD.

MRS. C. G. DUBOIS.

For six cups measure out four cupfuls of milk; put it in a basin, with one cupful of very strong coffee and one ounce powdered white sugar, and the yolks of five eggs; mix well and strain. Fill the cups with the mixture, skim off all froth from the surface, put them in a flat stew-pan of water, with live coals on its cover, or a very slow fire for fifteen minutes. The water should only bubble slightly; when set, let the cups cool in the water.

————:o:————

COCOANUT CUSTARD.

MRS. COL. SMITH.

One-half cupful of butter, one cupful of powdered sugar, four well-beaten eggs, one cupful of grated cocoanut and a quart of milk; mix butter and sugar together, and then add the eggs and cocoanut, and lastly the milk. Bake in a lower crust.

————:o:————

ORANGE SOUFFLE.

MRS. S. YARNELL.

Make a rich boiled custard of one quart of milk and the yolks of six eggs (reserving the whites for frosting); sweeten to taste; when cool, pour the juice of four or five oranges, sprinkled with sugar and the grated rind of two; cover with frosting; set in a pan of cold water, and set in the oven until a nice brown; to be eaten cold.

————:o:————

BAVARIAN CREAM.

MRS. J. G. EASTMAN.

Whip one pint of cream to a stiff froth. Boil one pint of rich milk with a vanilla bean and two tablespoonfuls of sugar until it is well flavored; then take it off the fire and add half a box of Cox's gelatine, soaked for an hour in half a cupful of water. When slightly cooled, stir in the yolks of four eggs, well beaten. When it has become quite cold, and begins to thicken, stir it until it is very smooth; then stir in the whipped cream until it is well mixed. Put it in a mold and set in a cool place to harden. It is very nice, eaten with whipped cream.

———:o:———

WHIPPED CREAM.

MRS. C. H. BRADLEY.

One pint of sweet cream; add one teacupful of white sugar, and one teaspoonful of lemon extract; beat the whole briskly until a stiff froth is formed. Then have ready a dish lined with slices of sponge-cake—stale is best. Take the froth in spoonfuls and lay it over the cake until the dish is full.

———:o:———

LEMON PUDDING SAUCE.

RELIABLE.

One lemon, the juice and half the peel grated, one heaping teacup of sugar, one-third of a cup of butter, one egg; beat well together the butter and sugar and egg, then the lemon and a little nutmeg; add, slowly, half a teacup of boiling water, but do not boil the sauce.

———:o:———

MY LEMON CUSTARD.

MRS. JOHN SMITH.

For each pie take three eggs, one small cupful of sugar, a lump of butter the size of a walnut, one dessert-spoon level full of corn-starch, and one lemon. Separate the eggs; put the yolks, sugar, butter, and corn-starch in a bowl, and mix well, adding the juice and grated rind of the lemon. Beat the whites very stiff and add to the custard, mixing all together, and pour into the crust and bake.

———:o:———

TAPIOCA SNOW.

MISS LILLIE MILLIKEN.

One teacupful of tapioca, soaked in four cupfuls of water over night. Add one cupful of sugar, the juice of one lemon, or the juice of three oranges. Boil until transparent; stir in while cooking the whites of four eggs, beaten to a froth; pour into a dish to cool. When cool, put strawberries over the top, and serve with cream and sugar. The fruit may be dispensed with.

————:o:————

BLANC MANGE.

MRS. COL. GEORGE SMITH.

Take one-half ounce of Irish moss, and cleanse in two or three waters. Boil it in one pint and a half of milk until reduced to a proper thickness; then sweeten and flavor to taste, and pour through a strainer into moulds.

————:o:————

MARYLAND FLOAT.

MRS. H. MCLELLAN.

Whites of four eggs, beaten very stiff; one cupful of powdered sugar, and add raspberry or any kind of jam, and beat until the fork will nearly stand alone in the mixture. Put in a glass bowl of soft custard, or milk, and then the float on top.

————:o:————

FLOATING ISLAND.

BERTHA LINDLEY.

One quart of milk and four eggs; beat whites and yolks separately; heat the milk; put in the whites and let them remain till cooked; then take out. Beat four tablespoonfuls of sugar with the yolks; pour into the milk; boil, and pour into a dish; flavor with lemon; put the whites on top, and set by to cool.

————:o:————

TAPIOCA CREAM.

MRS. C. H. BRADLEY.

One cupful of pearled tapioca; boil in four cupfuls of water until clear; then add the juice of one lemon and two cupfuls of white sugar. Beat the whites of four eggs to a stiff froth, and stir in while hot. To be eaten cold, with sweetened and flavored cream.

————:o:————

CHARLOTTE DE RUSSE.

MRS. L. S. E. LONGSTREET.

Five and a half ounces of sugar and two eggs (beat the sugar and yolks together, whites separately); one pint of sweet cream, beaten to a stiff froth, and one-third of a box of Cox's gelatine, dissolved in a tablespoonful of warm water. Add this to the sugar and eggs; flavor with vanilla; then add cream, and stir up quickly.

———:o:———

CHANTILLA CREAM.

MRS. W. WIDNEY.

To a pint of cream, beaten stiff, add the whites of two well-beaten eggs, a cup of sugar, and flavoring to taste. Cut squares of sponge-cake and lay alternately in a dish with the cream.

———:o:———

PUDDING SAUCE.

MRS. C. G. DU BOIS.

Stew a dozen plums or cherries; boil one pint of cream and pour it over a pound of sugar; add the fruit; flavor with lemon.

———:o:———

PUDDING SAUCE.

MRS. S. B. CASWELL.

Two-thirds of a cupful of butter, one cupful of sugar, and one tablespoonful of flour, beat to a cream. Stand it over the fire; stir in quickly three gills of water, and flavor.

———:o:———

TAPIOCA CREAM.

MRS. WRIGHT, SAN BERNARDINO.

Two large tablespoonfuls of tapioca; pour over it two tea-cupfuls of warm water; put it on the back of the stove and let soften gradually. Should the water be absorbed before the tapioca is soft, add a little more. After an hour or so pour it in a sauce-pan and add one pint of milk. When it begins to boil, add the yolks of three eggs, well beaten, sugar to taste, a tablespoonful of cold milk, to prevent the eggs from curdling, a little lemon flavoring, and a little salt. Let it boil a minute or two; then pour into a pudding dish, leaving an inch or two for a soft icing. For the icing, the whites of the eggs, beaten stiff, and pulverized sugar stirred in until quite stiff. Flavor with lemon; pour over the tapioca, place it in the oven, and let the icing harden very quickly, becoming a delicate brown. Then place in an ice-chest, or some cool place.

————:o:————

LIQUID SAUCE.

MRS. C. G. DU BOIS.

One tablespoonful of flour, two tablespoonfuls of sugar, a small piece of butter, nutmeg, and boiling water. Stir till cooked.

————:o:————

CHOCOLATE CREAM.

MRS. GEN. STONEMAN.

Two quarts of milk, boiled and sweetened, and three-quarters of a pound of chocolate, scraped, and dissolved in milk. Add the milk to the chocolate, stirring constantly, and boil till you think it is cooked. Beat the yolks of four eggs and add to the chocolate. When cool, strain the whole, and boil to the consistency of rich custard.

————:o:————

CHARLOTTE DE RUSSE.

MRS. E. C. STARIN.

Line a pan with lady's fingers, or nice pound-cake of any kind. Sweeten a quart of cream to taste and flavor with vanilla; then whip it. Pour a cupful of hot water on half an ounce of gelatine, and after it is dissolved, stir very hard into the whipped cream and pour into the mold. Be careful not to upset the cake.

————:o:————

CREAM SAUCE.

MRS. C. G. DU BOIS.

Boil half pint of cream; thicken it a very little; put in a small lump of butter, and sweeten to taste. After it gets cool, add flavoring. Good with boiled rice.

————:o:————

CREAM A' LA VANILLA.

MRS. GEORGE CLARK.

One ounce of gelatine, five ounces of sugar, three pints of fresh milk and one teaspoonful of extract of vanilla. After softening the gelatine by soaking it in cold water or milk, boil it in the milk till dissolved. Pour it, boiling hot, over the yolks of six eggs, after they have been beaten light and the sugar added. Return to the kettle and stir all rapidly together for about three minutes. Meanwhile have ready blanc mange molds, which have been dipped in cold water. Remove from the stove, and continue to stir the cream until nearly cold; then fill the molds and set them aside until stiff enough to turn out.

————:o:————

SPANISH CREAM.

MRS. JOHN FOY, SAN BERNARDINO.

Put a half box of gelatine in a quart of milk; let it soak from forty minutes to an hour; then put on the fire and stir until it is fully dissolved. Add the yolks of four eggs and four tablespoonfuls of sugar, well beaten together. Stir till it comes to the boiling point. Have ready the whites of four eggs and four tablespoonfuls of sugar, beaten to a froth. Remove from the stove, and add the whites and sugar thus prepared, stirring until thoroughly mixed; flavor to taste; put in the mold, and set in a cool place. If made in summer, it must be put on ice, or it will not separate. To be eaten with cream.

————:o:————

STRAWBERRY ICE CREAM.

MRS. MILLIKEN.

Beat four eggs with one pound of powdered sugar, add three pints of milk; set the dish in a kettle of hot water, constantly stirring until it thickens; set it away to cool. When cold, add five pints of cream, and strain through thin muslin into freezer. Fill the freezer one-third full of ice, with salt sprinkled in; turn very slowly ten minutes, then add one-third more ice, with salt; turn faster five minutes, then strain in three-fourths of a quart of strawberry juice, beaten with one-half a pound of powdered sugar; then turn as fast as possible for twenty minutes, draw off the water, pack and let it stand four hours. For vanilla or other flavorings leave out the half pound of sugar. Strawberries can be used in place of juice, if preferred.

SPANISH DEPARTMENT.

ESTOFADO.

MRS. J. G. DOWNEY.

Put into a saucepan a spoonful of lard; when hot, add two pounds of beef ribs or mutton—a chicken is best. Add some onions and green peppers, whole, a little garlic, cut very fine, black pepper, thyme, a little vinegar, a few raisins and olives, a few tomatoes, and four slices of toast. Cover close and stew slowly.

————:o:————

FRICASSEED TRIPE.

MRS. T. S. STANWAY.

Fry brown in butter one large onion. Cut a pound or more of tripe in narrow strips; put a small cupful of water to it; add a bit of butter the size of an egg, one large tomato, with the skin removed and cut up fine, two or three chilis, seeded, one hard-boiled egg, one tablespoonful of vinegar, pepper, salt, a little nutmeg, and one teaspoonful of sugar. Let it simmer gently for an hour, and serve hot.

————:o:————

MEAT PUDDING.

MRS. J. G. DOWNEY.

Boil four pounds of brisket; when done, remove the bone and cut into slices. Have ready some prepared dry peppers; throw the meat into the pepper and let it simmer a few minutes; add salt and onion. While simmering make a batter of one quart of corn meal, one tablespoonful of butter, and two teaspoonfuls of baking-powder. Make the batter very stiff. Add some raisins, olives, and salt; spread out on a pudding-cloth, and put the meat in the center of the batter, reserving some of the pepper-sauce for serving.

Tie the cloth securely, and boil the pudding in the liquor the meat was boiled in.

To prepare the dried peppers for the pudding: Take two dozen dried peppers, and remove the seeds and veins; wash them, and put enough cold water on them to just cover them. Place them in a saucepan on the stove and let come to a boil; take from the fire; when cold drain the water off, but do not throw it away. Pound the soaked peppers with a potato-masher for about ten minutes; add about one-third of the water they were boiled in; stir well, and strain through a colander. The strained liquor should be of the consistency of thick gravy. A little garlic may be added, if the taste is not disagreeable.

————:o:————

ROAST GOOSE A' LA ESPANOLA.

RELIABLE.

Select a young and tender goose; dress and draw one day previous to using; season well with salt and pepper inside and out; hang in a dry, cool place till next day. Prepare the following stuffing: Four ounces of bread crumbs, and one onion, chopped fine with gizzard, liver, and heart; rub well together, adding half teaspoonful of good black pepper, some salt and finely-powdered sage. Mix well together with a fork, adding slowly two heaping tablespoonfuls of melted butter and one egg, beaten to a froth; fill the inside and neck of the goose, sewing the openings together with needle and thread; place in a deep dripping-pan, with two tablespoonfuls of butter rubbed all over the goose, and one teacupful of warm water; dredge well with flour and bake in a slow oven, allowing fifteen minutes for each pound of weight. Serve with hot apple or onion sauce.

————:o:————

TO STUFF PEPPERS.

MRS. J. G. DOWNEY.

Take a dozen large peppers; remove the seeds; then throw them upon a bed of live coals and turn continually until they are a light brown. When taking them up, throw them immediately into a bowl of cold water and remove the skins. Put a tablespoonful of lard or butter into a saucepan, and when hot add an onion, finely chopped; fry slightly; add a large tomato, or two if small, half teacupful of grated corn; pepper and salt to taste. Let it simmer fifteen minutes, stirring occasionally to prevent scorching; then remove from the fire; add a heaped teacupful of finely chopped meat or chicken (a small piece of ham' or bacon greatly improves its flavor); mix well, and stuff the peppers; dip into batter and fry to a nice brown.

Another way: Prepare the peppers as in the foregoing recipe. Put into a saucepan a spoonful of lard. When hot add one onion, and fry a little; add two teacupfuls of chopped meat, two tomatoes, if small, two peppers, chopped, a little black pepper, thyme, and salt. Fry a few minutes, and then stuff the Chilis. Dip into batter and fry.

Sauce for the peppers: Put a spoonful of butter into a saucepan; add a spoonful of flour, one onion, one tomato. one green pepper, cut small, two apples, sliced, a few raisins, if liked, and olives. Add enough water to make a sauce, and let it boil until the apples are done. Before serving the peppers, put them into the gravy and let it simmer just a moment; then serve.

———:o:———

CHILI (SPANISH) ZALZA, SAUCE PIQUANT.

RELIABLE.

Take four large tomatoes, removing the tops and ends, one large silver-skin onion, and four large-sized green Chili peppers, removing the seed; chop fine and drain five minutes through a colander; place in a deep dish; season to taste, with salt, black pepper, vinegar, and best Lucca oil. To be served with either hot or cold meats. Olives may be added before serving, if acceptable.

———:o:———

STUFFING FOR DUCKS, CHICKENS, OR OTHER FOWLS.

MRS. J. G. DOWNEY.

Take the gizzards, livers, and a piece of lean beef, and boil them; afterwards, when cold, chop them up fine. Take a small onion, two green Chilis, and a medium-sized tomato; cut them up fine. Then take a tablespoonful of lard or fresh butter and put in a frying-pan; fry for a few seconds, and then add the above ingredients; stir for a little while; then add a half teacupful of vinegar and a half cupful of pure water; add a little sugar and browned flour, a dozen olives, half cupful of raisins, and two hard-boiled eggs, choppod fine. Stir up together, and cover until the mass obtains consistency, when it is ready for use.

————:o:————

SOPA ESPANOLA.

RELIABLE.

Four pounds of lean veal and one-quarter of a pound of best salt pork. Place the veal in a stew-pan, covering well with cold water, and let it simmer slowly four hours. In the meantime chop the pork separately in fine pieces, and fry a light brown; add this to the contents of the stew-pan. One hour before serving, add two turnips, one small-sized onion, one carrot and one beet, all sliced. Cook slowly forty minutes; then remove the meat, strain the broth through a colander, and place again in the stew-pan with four table-spoonfuls of the best oat meal. Cook twenty minutes; add one teacupful of cream, half a nutmeg, grated, half tea-spoonful of alspice, and pepper and salt to taste. Pour into the tureen in which place previously toasted bread, cut in dice at pleasure. Serve hot.

————:o:————

SQUASH AND CORN.

MRS. J. G. DOWNEY.

Take three squashes and three ears of corn; chop the squashes and cut the corn from the cobs. Put into a sauce-pan a spoonful of lard or butter, and when very hot add an onion; fry a little; add the corn and squash, one tomato, one green pepper, cut small, and salt to taste. Cover closely, and stir frequently to prevent scorching.

CAKE DEPARTMENT.

—:o:—

COCOANUT CAKE.

MRS. R. M. WIDNEY.

One cupful of sugar, four eggs, one small half cupful of butter, one third cupful of sweet milk, and one pint of sifted flour. Bake the cake in layers.

Custard for the cake: One-half pint of sweet milk and one egg. Make a custard and thicken with cocoanut; place between the layers quite thick. Make an icing of the white of one egg and half tablespoonful of powdered sugar, and spread over the top layer; then sprinkle on dry cocoanut. Do not dry the icing before sprinkling on the cocoanut. Use Schepp's cocoanut.

—:o:—

HARRISON CAKE.

MRS. DR. ROSS.

One cupful brown sugar, one cupful molasses, one cupful butter, one cupful milk, three eggs, and three cupfuls flour, slightly browned. Mix into the flour one teaspoonful yeast-powder, and into the molasses one teaspoonful of soda. Add one cupful of chopped raisins, one of currants, and one of citron. Season with allspice, cinnamon, cloves and mace; teaspoonful of each. This is a delicious cake—almost equal to the richest fruit cake.

—:o:—

NUT CAKE.

MRS. I. W. HELLMAN.

One-half cupful butter, one-half cupful sugar, three eggs, two and a half cupfuls flour, one and a half teaspoonfuls baking powder, one-half cupful milk, one cupful chopped walnuts. Rub the butter and sugar to a light, white cream; add the eggs, beaten a little, then the flour, sifted with the powder; mix with the milk and nuts into a rather firm batter. Bake thirty-five minutes, and try with a straw.

————:o:————

EXCELLENT GINGER SNAPS.

MRS. GILLETTE.

Two cupfuls molasses, one cupful butter and lard mixed, two teaspoonfuls saleratus, one egg. Boil molasses and the cupful of shortening together five minutes; let cool a few minutes, then stir in the beaten egg and salaratus, holding it over the pan of flour while stirring it in, as it will foam and run over. As much ginger as is liked. Mix thin, roll thin. A few minutes will bake them. These are excellent.

————:o:————

EMMA'S JUMBLES.

MRS. C. G. DU BOIS.

Weigh one-half pound butter, three-quarter pounds flour, one-half pound powdered sugar (put by a little sugar to roll them in). Beat two eggs well; add little nut-meg. Make this into a stff dough; do not roll, but break off pieces the size of walnuts, and make into rings; lay them in tins to bake, an inch apart, as it runs and spreads. A moderate oven.

————:o:————

ORANGE CAKE.

MISS LILLIE MILLIKEN.

Two small cupfuls of sugar and half cupful of butter, worked to a cream; then add three well-beaten eggs, one cupful of milk, three cupfuls of flour, and two teaspoonfuls of baking-powder; bake in five jelly-tins in a quick oven. For frosting to put between the cakes, use the whites of two eggs, the juice and grated rind of one orange, and sugar enough to make it quite stiff.

————:o:————

CREAM CAKE.

MRS. O. W. CHILDS.

Four eggs, one cupful of sugar, one cupful of flour, one teaspoonful of yeast-powder, and a pinch of salt. Pour the above mixture into jelly-cake pans, and bake a light brown in a quick oven.

Cream custard for the above cake, to be used the same as for jelly cake: One pint of milk, one tablespoonful of corn-starch, one egg, two heaping tablespoonfuls of white sugar, and one teaspoonful of butter. Flavor with vanilla. Bring the milk and sugar almost to a boil; then add the corn-starch, stirred smooth with a little milk, and a pinch of salt. Stir it at the back of the range for five minutes, not allowing it to boil. Take it off and let cool a little; then stir in the egg well, and put the kettle on the fire again for a few minutes. Add the flavoring, and spread thick on the layers of cake. Ice the upper layer.

———:o:———

WHITE CAKE.

MRS. J. W. GILLETTE.

One cupful butter, two cupfuls white sugar, whites of six eggs, beaten light, one-half cupful of milk, with a lump of soda the size of a pea, and three cupfuls of flour. Flavor to taste, lemon or almond.

——— – :o:———

CREAM SPONGE CAKE.

MRS. J. YARNELL.

One cupful sifted flour, one cupful granulated sugar, four eggs; beat the yolks and sugar thoroughly, then add the whites, beating again, then flour very lightly. Bake in layers in a quick oven. Make the cream with a little milk, the white of one egg, and sufficient corn-starch to make it the con-sistency of thick cream; sweeten and flavor to taste.

———:o:———

PENNSYLVANIA SPONGE CAKE.

MRS. I. R. DUNKELBERGER.

Seven eggs, one pound of white sugar, three-quarters of a pound of flour, and one gill of warm water. Put the sugar into a vessel and pour the water over it; stand it where it will keep warm—not hot; break the eggs into a tin bucket and pour the heated sugar on it, beating with the egg-beater as you pour it; keep the bucket containing the sugar and eggs over a vessel of hot water all the time you beat. Continue this half an hour; then stir in very lightly the flavoring and flour, and bake immediately in a buttered tin.

————:o:————

BRIDE'S CAKE.

MRS. M. M. TEMPLETON.

Half cupful of butter, two cupfuls of white sugar, the whites of five eggs, one cupful of sweet milk, three cupfuls of flour, and two teaspoonfuls of baking-powder. Flavor to taste.

————:o:————

CORN–STARCH CAKE.

MRS. J. HINES.

Two cupfuls sugar, one cupful butter, one-half cupful milk, whites of six eggs. Beat to a foam. Two teaspoonfuls of cream of tartar, one cupful of soda, two cupfuls flour, one cupful corn-starch.

————:o:————

SNOW SPONGE CAKE.

MRS. J. W. GILLETTE.

One cupful of flour, a little heated, one and a half cupfuls sugar, two teaspoonfuls cream of tartar mixed with flour, (no soda,) whites of ten eggs. This makes a very white, beautiful cake.

————:o:————

DOUGHNUTS.

MRS. J. YARNELL.

Piece of butter the size of a walnut, one cupful sugar, two eggs, one-half cupful sweet milk, two teaspoonfuls baking powder, flour enough to make into a stiff dough. This makes but a few, and they are very nice.

————:o:————

ORANGE CAKE.

MRS. DR. ROSS.

One cupful of powdered sugar, one and a half cupfuls of flour, half cupful of sweet milk, a lump of butter the size of a walnut, one egg and the yolk of another, and one heaping teaspoonful of yeast-powder. Bake in three layers, as for jelly cake. Take the white of one egg, beaten to a stiff froth, to which add the grated rind and the juice of one orange and three tablespoonfuls of sugar. Spread this between the cakes as you would jelly.

————:o:————

COFFEE CAKE.

MRS. J. HINES.

Two cupfuls sugar, one cupful butter, six eggs, one cupful cold, strong coffee, two cups raisins, one cupful currants, two teaspoonfuls cream of tartar, one cupful soda, one dessert-spoonful of mace; spice to taste.

————:o:————

CRULLERS.

MRS. M. M. BOVARD.

Four eggs, four tablespoonfuls of sugar, three tablespoonfuls of melted butter or lard, and four tablespoonfuls of flour. Roll thin, cut in two-inch squares, and slit in six bars, one under and one over the finger. Fry in hot lard.

————:o:—— –

VELVET SPONGE CAKE.

MRS. DR. FRENCH.

Four eggs, two cupfuls sugar, two cupfuls flour, two-thirds of a cupful boiling water; add the water last; one teaspoonful of baking powder, one teaspoonful of essence of lemon.

————:o:—————

DELICATE CAKE.

MRS. C. G. DU BOIS.

Whites of eight eggs, three cupfuls sugar, one cupful butter, one-half cupful sweet milk, four cupfuls flour, four teaspoonfuls of baking-powder.

————:o:————

LEMON CAKE.

MRS. J. W. GILLETTE.

One cupful sugar, one-half cupful butter, two cupfuls flour, two eggs, one-half cupful milk, one teaspoonful cream baking powder, lemon essence. For the jelly: Take coffee-cupful sugar, two tablespoonfuls butter, two eggs, juice of two lemons. Beat all together, and boil until the consistency of jelly. Orange may be used in the same way. For orange and lemon pies, add one teaspoonful of corn-starch to the above.

————:o:————

BOSTON GINGER–BREAD.

MISS M. E. HOYT.

One pound of flour, half a pound of butter, six eggs, a little brown sugar, one pint of molasses, and half a teacupful of ginger, to which add nutmeg, cinnamon, or any other flavoring, to taste; also, one teaspoonful of soda, dissolved in a little vinegar.

————:o:————

COFFEE CAKE.

MRS. G. W. WELLS.

One cupful of sugar, one cupful of molasses, one cupful of cold coffee, two cupfuls of raisins, one cupful of melted butter, two eggs, two teaspoonfuls of baking-powder, half teaspoonful of cinnamon, and cloves and nutmeg. Bake one hour.

————:o:————

GINGER NUTS.

RELIABLE.

One cupful of molasses, one cupful of sugar, one cupful of butter, two teaspoonfuls of ginger, two teaspoonfuls of baking-powder, and sufficient flour to make a stiff dough. Roll thin, cut out, and bake in a quick oven.

————:o:————

COOKIES.

MRS. A. W. POTTS.

Two cupfuls of sugar, one cupful of butter, one cupful of cold water, and half teaspoonful of soda.

————:o:————

POUND CAKE.

MRS. S. SPEEDY.

One light pound of butter, beat to a cream; twelve eggs, beat these well; one light pound of powdered sugar, add this to the butter, and beat ten minutes; add the eggs and beat five minutes; one light pound of sifted flour; set this in the oven and make it warm; mix this in very lightly, barely enough to mix; bake in a moderate oven one hour. I find this is much easier and nicer stirred with the hand.

———:o:———

SILVER CAKE.

MRS. J. HINES.

Two cupfuls of sugar, one cupful of butter, one cupful of milk, the whites of eight eggs, two teaspoonfuls of cream of tartar, one of soda, and four cupfuls of flour.

———:o:———

NUT CAKE.

MRS. W. D. GIBBS.

One cupful of sugar, one cupful of cream, one-third of a cupful of butter, two eggs, one teaspoonful of soda, two teaspoonfuls of cream of tartar, dissolved in two spoonfuls of milk, and one cupful of nuts.

———:o:———

CHOCOLATE CAKE.

MRS. M. M. BOVARD.

Two cupfuls of sugar, one cupful of butter, the yolks of five eggs and the whites of two, one cupful of milk, three and a half cupfuls of flour, half teaspoonful of soda, and one teaspoonful of cream of tartar, sifted in the flour. Bake in jelly-cake tins.

Mixture for filling: The whites of three eggs, half a cupful of sugar, three tablespoonfuls of grated chocolate, and one teaspoonful of vanilla. Beat together, and spread between the layers.

———:o:———

MARBLE CAKE.

MRS. J. M. STEWART.

White Portion: Seven eggs (white only), two cupfuls white sugar, one cupful butter, three cupfuls flour, one and a half cupfuls milk, one teaspoonful soda, two teaspoonfuls cream of tartar.

Dark Portion: Seven eggs (yolks only), one cupful butter, two cupfuls brown sugar, one cupful syrup, one cupful sour cream, five cupfuls flour, one teaspoonful nutmeg, two teaspoonfuls cinnamon, one teaspoonful soda. Combine to represent marble.

———:o:———

GERMAN CHRISTMAS CAKE.

MRS. A. HIGBIE, COMPTON.

Two cupfuls of honey and one cupful of sugar; put on the stove to boil; add walnuts or almonds, and a lemon peel, cut fine. Let it cool a little, and add spices, cloves, nutmeg, etc. When quite cool, stir in the flour, in which has been mixed a teaspoonful of baking-powder; then add citron. Roll it out and cut in squares, to bake the same day or the next.

———:o:———

GINGER–SNAPS.

MRS. J. M. STEWART.

One cupful of butter, one cupful of syrup, one and one-half cupfuls of brown sugar, one tablespoonful of cinnamon, one tablespoonful of ginger, one teaspoonful of soda, dissolved in four tablespoonfuls of water; flour enough to roll.

———:o:———

GOLD CAKE.

MRS. J. HINES.

Two cupfuls of sugar, one cupful of butter, one cupful of milk, the yolks of eight eggs, two teaspoonfuls of cream of tartar, one of soda, and four cupfuls of flour.

———:o:———

CREAM CAKE.

MRS. A. W. POTTS.

Three-quarters of a cupful of milk, half cupful of powdered sugar, a lump of butter half the size of an egg, and one tablespoonful of corn-starch. Boil the milk, butter, and sugar together; add the corn-starch, wet with a little cold milk; stir briskly while boiling. Boil from three to five minutes. When cold, flavor to taste.

Cream for the cake: One cupful of sugar, half tablespoonful of butter, three eggs, half cupful of flour, half cupful of corn-starch, and one teaspoonful of Dooley's yeast-powders. Bake in jelly-cake tins, and put together one hour before serving, substituting the cream for jelly. The above is for a small cake. If your jelly-cake tins are large, double the quantities for cake and cream.

———:o:———

LAFAYETTE CAKE.

MRS. J. M. STEWART.

Two cupfuls of sugar, one-half cupful of butter, beat to a light cream; four cupfuls of flour, one cupful of sweet milk, three eggs, two teaspoonfuls of creamtartar, one teaspoonful of soda.

———:o:———

GINGER COOKIES.

MRS. A. N. HAMILTON.

One cupful of butter, one cupful of sugar, two cupfuls of molasses, one tablespoonful alum, dissolved in two-thirds of a cupful of boiling water; two teaspoonfuls of soda, dissolved in the same quantity of boiling water; Ginger to taste.

———:o:———

PORK CAKE.

MRS. G. W. WELLS.

One pound of salt pork, chopped fine; one pint of hot water, one pound of raisins, two cupfuls of sugar and one of molasses, one tablespoonful of soda, one tablespoonful of cloves, one tablespoonful of cinnamon, five cupfuls of flour.

———:o:———

WHITE CAKE.

MRS. L. CHEEK.

Three-fourths of a cupful of butter, two cupfuls of sugar, one cupful of sweet milk, the whites of four eggs, and four cupfuls of flour, in which two teaspoonfuls of baking-powder has been mixed. Flavor with lemon.

———:o:———

SPONGE JELLY CAKE—ROLLED.

MRS. JOHN FOY, SAN BERNARDINO.

Five eggs, one cupful of sugar, one cupful of flour, and two teaspoonfuls of baking-powder. Beat the yolks and sugar to a cream; add the whites, beaten to a stiff froth; then the flour, in which the baking-powder has been well mixed. Bake in a dripping-pan. When done, turn out in a cloth, spread jelly on the bottom of the cake, and roll from the side. Sprinkle sugar over the top. This cake may be cut in slices and served, with a sweet sauce, for dessert.

———:o:———

CUP CAKE.

MRS. A. A. DODSWORTH.

Four eggs, one and one-half cupfuls of sugar, three table-spoonfuls of butter, one and one-half teaspoonfuls of Royal baking-powder, two cupfuls of flour, nutmeg if you like, milk to make the right thickness.

———:o:———

COCOANUT CAKES.

MRS. GEN. STONEMAN.

To the whites of six eggs one pound of loaf sugar; mix a pound of the cocoanut, or sufficient to make a stiff paste. Flour your hands and make it up into little balls; lay them on buttered white paper, grate sugar over them, and bake in brisk oven.

———:o:———

ICING.

MRS. F. D. BOVARD.

The whites of two eggs, twelve even tablespoonfuls of pulverized sugar; beat the eggs to a stiff froth. This will frost two good sized cakes.

———:o:———

CITRON CAKE.

MRS. J. E. HOLLENBECK.

Take the whites of twelve eggs, three cupfuls of sugar, one small cupful of butter, a cupful of sweet milk, four small cupfuls of flour, half a cupful of corn-starch, two tea-spoonfuls of baking-powder, and lemon to taste, adding a cupful of citron, sliced thin and dusted with flour.

———:o:———

BOILED SPONGE CAKE.

MRS. CHARLES MACLAY, SAN FERNANDO.

Three-quarters of a pound of sugar, seven eggs, and half pound of flour. Beat whites and yolks separately; then put them together; a few minutes before doing so put sugar on the stove, with half a teacupful of water; let it come to a good boil, and pour it on the eggs, stirring all the while until cold; then add flour and flavoring; try with a splint when done.

————:o:————

GINGER COOKIES.

MRS. S. B. CASWELL.

Two cupfuls of molasses, one cupful of butter, five cupfuls of flour, or enough to roll out very soft; add ginger to taste. Keep air tight.

————:o:————

COLD WATER CAKE.

MISS MARY MCLELLAN.

One cupful of butter, two cupfuls of sugar, one cupful of cold water, four cupfuls of flour, one cupful of seeded raisins, three eggs, two teaspoonfuls of baking powder. Flavor with nutmeg or mace. Beat all at once.

————:o:————

SPICE CAKE.

MRS. G. W. WELLS.

Six eggs, leave out the whites of two; one cupful of butter, two cupfuls of brown sugar, one cupful of sweet milk, one tablespoonful of allspice, one teaspoonful of every kind of spice, three teaspoonfuls of baking powder; flour sufficient to make proper stiffness.

————:o:————

COOKIES.

MRS. J. M. STEWART.

One cupful of butter, one cupful of sour cream, two cupfuls of sugar, three eggs, one teaspoonful of soda, and caraway seed if you like.

————:o:————

CREAM CAKES.

MRS. H. K. S. O'MELVENY.

To one quart of cream add one pound of butter. Before mixing cream the butter and whip the cream. Add enough flour and a little salt to make a dough stiff enough to roll.

Cut off a small piece, roll it out with your hand, then bring both ends to the center, making two loops. Have ready on your breadboard some granulated sugar, lay the cake on it, and press it down with the rolling-pin. Put the cakes in a dripping pan, with the sugar side up, and bake.

———:o:———

CUP CAKE.

MRS. J. E. HOLLENBECK.

Three cupfuls of flour, two of sugar, one of butter, one-third of a cupful of cream, five eggs, well beaten, two teaspoonfuls of cream of tartar and one of soda, dissolved separately. Mix all well together, and bake in a moderate oven.

———:o:———

DELICATE CAKE.

MRS. G. W. WELLS.

Whites of four eggs, beaten to a stiff froth; one-half cupful of butter, and one cupful of sugar, stirred to a cream; one-half cupful of sweet milk, one cupful of flour, one teaspoonful cream of tartar, one-half teaspoonful of soda, three tablespoonfuls of cornstarch.

———:o:———

JELLY CAKE.

MRS. DR. FRENCH.

One cupful of sugar, a lump of butter the size of an egg, three eggs, one cupful of flour, one teaspoonful of cream of tartar, and a half teaspoonful of soda, dissolved in one tablespoonful of milk. Bake in jelly-cake tins. When cold, spread jelly between the layers.

———:o:———

WALNUT CAKE.

MRS. GEORGE CLARK.

One cupful of milk, three-quarters of a cupful of butter, two cupfuls of granulated sugar, three cupfuls of flour, two teaspoonfuls of baking-powder, three eggs, and not quite a cupful of kernels of walnuts, broken up. In the first place beat the butter and sugar to a cream; next stir the milk in slowly; then beat separately the yolks and whites of the eggs; add the yolks, the butter, and sugar; then the whites, beaten to a stiff froth; stir all well together; next sift in the flour, putting the broken nuts in last. Bake in square pans. Frost both cakes with icing, and put one cake on top of the other. Divide the frosting into small squares, laying half a nut in the middle of each square.

————:o:————

MOUNTAIN CAKE.

MRS. G. W. WELLS.

Two cupfuls of butter, two cupfuls of sugar, four eggs, whites and yolks beaten separately; three and one-half cupfuls of flour, one cupful of sweet milk, two teaspoonfuls of cream of tartar, one teaspoonful of soda.

————:o:————

HONEY CAKE.

MRS. I. W. HELLMAN.

One cupful of honey, one-half cupful of butter, mix them well together; three eggs, three-quarters of a cupful of black coffee, three pieces of grated chocolate, one-half teaspoonful of cinnamon and allspice. To every cupful of flour take a teaspoonful of yeast powder, and enough flour to make a very stiff batter; one-half cupful of citron, one cupful of stoned raisins, and one-half cupful of almonds.

————:o:————

CHOCOLATE CAKE.

MRS. J. E. HOLLENBECK.

Take one cupful of butter, two of sugar, one of milk, five eggs, leaving out the whites of three, four cupfuls of sifted flour, and two teaspoonfuls of baking-powder; bake in three or four layers. For icing, take the whites of three eggs, beaten stiff, one and a half cupfuls of powdered sugar, six tablespoonfuls of grated chocolate, and two teaspoonfuls of vanilla.

————:o:————

BACHELORS' BUTTONS.

MRS. S. B. CASWELL.

These are small cakes about the size of maccaroons. They are very nice. One cupful of white sugar, half cupful of butter, one and a half cupfuls of flour, and one egg; flavor with almond. Roll into little balls about the size of a small walnut; then roll them in white sugar and put into buttered pans some distance apart, to allow them to flatten out. Add a little more flour if they flatten too much. This recipe should make between fifty and sixty.

————:o:————

CUP POUND CAKE.

MISS A. E. WIDNEY.

Two and one-half cupfuls of sugar, three-quarters of a cupful of butter, six eggs, one cupful of milk, three and one-half cupfuls of sifted flour, two teaspoonfuls of yeast powder, two teaspoonfuls of vanilla.

————:o:————

ANGEL CAKE.

RELIABLE.

Take one large cupful of flour, add to it a teaspoonful of cream of tartar; sift through a sieve four times. Beat to a stiff froth the whites of eleven eggs, add to them slowly, as in making frosting, one and a half cupfuls of pulverized sugar, and one teaspoonful of extract of vanilla; then stir in the flour, sifting it slowly through the fingers. Bake in a deep unbuttered tin, and do not remove from the tin till quite cold.

————:o:————

ORANGE CAKE.

MISS A. TUTHILL.

Two cupfuls of sugar and one-half cupful of butter, creamed, one cupful of sweet milk, three eggs, well beaten, and three teaspoonfuls of baking-powder. Mix with three cupfuls of flour. Bake in four layers.

Filling: Grate the rind of one large orange; squeeze out the juice; mix with one cupful of sugar, one egg, and one tablespoonful of cocoanut, or not, as you please. Boil this about two minutes, and spread between the layers.

————:o:————

CREAM CAKES.

MRS. J. C. NEWTON, SAN GABRIEL.

For the outside: One pint of water, half pound of butter, three-quarters of a pound of flour, and ten eggs. Boil the water and butter together; stir in the flour while boiling; take it from the fire to cool; when cold, add the eggs by breaking them into the mixture one at a time; stir them in very thoroughly, but be sure not to beat them; add a teaspoonful of cold water; drop them into your pan; form them with a spoon, as they do not rise much. Bake fifteen or twenty minutes in a hot oven, and do not open the door until they are done.

Mixture for the inside: Two cupfuls of sugar, one cupful of flour, one pint of milk, and four eggs. Boil the milk; beat the eggs, sugar and flour together, and stir them into the milk while boiling, until thickened. Next add essence of lemon, to flavor, and when the mixture is cool, fill your cakes.

————:o:————.

CREAM SPONGE CAKE.

MRS. H. C. AUSTIN.

One cupful of sugar, two eggs, one-half cupful of cream, one cupful of flour, one teaspoonful of yeast powder. Beat sugar and eggs light; add the cream, and lastly, flour and powder.

————:o:————

RICH CRULLERS.

MISS M. E. HOYT.

Four pounds of flour, one pound of butter, one-quarter pound of lard, ten eggs, one and one-quarter pounds of sugar.

————:o:————

COCOANUT CAKE.

MRS. I. S. SMITH.

One pound of fine sugar, half pound of butter, three-quarters of a pound of flour, one large cocoanut, grated, six eggs, whites and yolks beaten separately, half cupful of milk, or the milk from the nut, if good, and three teaspoonfuls of baking-powder. Stir the butter and sugar to a cream; then add the yolks and other ingredients, and just before placing in the oven add the cocoanut.

————:o:————

BOSTON CREAM CAKE.

MISS A. TUTHILL.

Paste: One cupful of water, two large tablespoonfuls of butter, one cupful of flour, and three eggs. Boil the water and butter together; stir in the flour while boiling, and let it cook a moment; when cool, add first the yolks, then the whites, well beaten. Drop with a spoon on buttered tins, forming little cakes some distance apart. Bake in a quick oven; they will puff in baking. When cold, cut one side large enough to insert the cream with a spoon.

Cream: One tablespoonful of cornstarch, two tablespoonfuls of sugar, one egg, and flavoring. Make like any other custard, and use cold.

————:o:————

[In these recipes for fruit cake, the glass of wine or brandy usually added for the preservation of the cake we omit.]

FRUIT CAKE.

MRS. O. W. CHILDS.

One pound of white sugar, one pound of butter, one pound of flour, twelve eggs, two pounds of seeded raisins, two pounds of currants, two pounds of citron, cut fine, and two grated nutmegs. Mix the butter and sugar together to a cream; add the yolks, well beaten, and then the whites, whipped to a stiff froth; mix the flour lightly, and then add the fruit and nutmeg. Bake two hours in a moderate oven.

————:o:————

FRUIT CAKE.

MRS. STAFFORD, SANTA ANA.

One and a half pounds of flour, one and a quarter pounds of brown sugar, one pound of butter, two pounds of seeded raisins, two pounds of currants, one and a half pounds of sliced citron, eleven eggs, two nutmegs, cloves, cinnamon, one teaspoonful of soda, and one cupful of molasses. Reserve one-third of the flour to mix with the fruit.

————:o:————

TUTTI FRUITTI CAKE.

MRS. J. G. HOWARD.

One cupful of butter, two cupfuls of sugar, one cupful of sweet milk, two and a half cupfuls of flour, good round measure, the whites of seven eggs, three teaspoonfuls of yeast-powder, one pound of raisins, one pound of figs, one pound of dates, one pound of almonds, and one pound of citron. Blanch the almonds and slice them in fine slices—

do not chop them; bake in two long tin pans, as you would sponge cake, the width just right for a slice; bake in a slow oven about one hour and three-quarters.

———:o:———

FRUIT CAKE.

MRS. IDA WIDNEY.

One pound of flour, one pound of sugar, one pound of butter, ten eggs, three pounds of seeded raisins, two pounds of currants, three quarters of a pound of citron, one ounce each of cinnamon, nutmeg, allspice and cloves, and half pint of molasses.

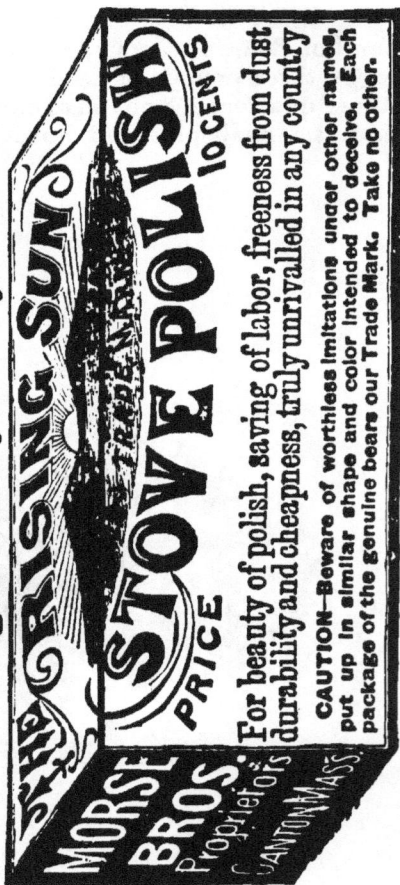

FRUIT DEPARTMENT,

ORANGES FILLED WITH JELLY.

MRS. I. R. DUNKELBERGER.

Select large oranges, and from the top of each remove with a sharp penknife a piece the size of a quarter of a dollar; then, with the handle of a teaspoon, take out the pulp, being careful not to break the rinds, and throw them into cold water. Press the juice from the pulp, strain (allow one ounce of white isinglass to six oranges); put the juice and isinglass over the fire, stir constantly, and boil four or five minutes. Color half the jelly a bright rose color, with red currant jelly, or cranberry jelly. Drain, and wipe the rinds, and when the jelly is quite cold, fill with alternate stripes of the two colored jellies. When perfectly cold, cut into quarters, with a very sharp knife, and arrange tastefully in a glass dish. This makes a beautiful ornamental dish for the dinner table.

————:o:————

ORANGE MARMALADE.

RELIABLE.

Nine bitter, three sweet oranges, four lemons. Cut the fruit across the grain, in the thinnest slices possible. Let it stand for thirty-six hours in four quarts of spring water. Boil for two hours; add eight pounds of white sugar, and boil for one hour, or until it jellies.

Lemon marmalade can be made in the same way.

————:o:————

PEAR PRESERVES.

MRS. H. MCLELLAN.

Parboil the fruit in just enough water to cover them. When done, place the pears on a plate; then take as many pounds of sugar of pears (before they were boiled), and place the sugar in the water the pears were boiled in. When it comes to a boil, drop in the pears and cook until they are soft enough not to fall in pieces.

————:o:————

PRESERVED FIGS.

MRS. W. W. WIDNEY.

Peel four pounds of white figs and add three pounds of sugar. Cook the same as other preserves.

————:o:————

POTTED PEACHES.

MRS. M. G. MOORE.

Four pounds of fruit and one pound of sugar. Make a syrup of water and the sugar, put the peaches into it, and cook about the same as for canning; after which, spread the fruit on a dish, boil the syrup very thick, and as the fruit dries, moisten with the syrup on both sides. Do this several times, and when about half dry, put the fruit into jars and pour the warm syrup over it. The syrup must be warm when moistening the fruit. Stew before using.

————:o:————

LEMON JELLY.

MRS. ADELIA HALL.

One-half box of gelatine soaked in one-half pint of water, juice of five large lemons, two cupfuls of loaf sugar, or sugar to taste; beaten white and shell of an egg, one and one-half pints of boiling water. Soak the gelatine in one pint of water half an hour. Rub several of the pieces of sugar over the peel of the lemon to soak the oil on the surface. Pour a pint and a half of boiling water on the soaked gelatine, and add lemon-juice, sugar, and egg; let it come to a boil, and set it on one side of the range for a few minutes, then skim carefully and pass through the jelly-bag.

————:o:————

GRAPE JELLY.

MRS. R. M. WIDNEY.

Wash your grapes the evening before making your jelly, to be sure they are perfectly dry before cooking them. Pick the small bunches from the main stem, put them in a porcelain kettle, and cook very soft; then turn into a flannel bag to drain. To one pint of the juice thus obtained add a pint of sugar, and boil twenty minutes. Never jelly a larger quantity than a pint in the same vessel at the same time.

————:o:————

RASPBERRY OR BLACKBERRY JAM.

MRS. COL. GEO. SMITH.

To every pound of fruit weigh three-quarters of a pound of crushed sugar. Put the sugar into the oven to heat, but not melt, while the fruit is cooking. Cook the fruit twenty minutes, and then add the hot sugar, and let it boil ten minutes longer, stirring constantly after the sugar ⌐oes in.

————:o:————

SPICED GOOSEBERRIES.

MRS. C. G. DU BOIS.

Five pounds of gooseberries and two and a half pounds of brown sugar. Boil from two to three hours. One-half hour before done, add one pint of vinegar, one and a half ounces of cloves, and one ounce of cinnamon. Stir while cooking.

————:o:————

ORANGE MARMALADE.

MRS. J. E. HOLLENBECK.

Grate off the outside or yellow peel of each orange and rub on salt as long as they will absorb it; put them in a gallon jar, add two cupfuls of salt, and pour boiling water over them once each day for three consecutive days. Then boil in fresh water for two hours; put in cold water until cool; quarter, remove the seeds and white pulp, and slice fine. Take equal weights of oranges and white sugar, and cook two hours in a preserve kettle, stirring frequently.

————:o:————

SPICED PEACHES.

MRS. S. C. HUBBELL.

To nine pounds of peaches add four and a half pounds of sugar, one pint of vinegar, and a half cupful each of cloves and cinnamon, tied in separate cloths. Pare and halve the peaches, and put them in a jar. Boil the vinegar, spice and sugar together for a few moments, and pour over the peaches boiling hot. Let them stand over night, and in the morning put all in a kettle and boil ten minutes. Take out the peaches, leaving the spice, and boil the vinegar until it begins to thicken; then pour it over the peaches.

----:o:----

CANNED QUINCES.

MRS. JOHN FOY, SAN BERNARDINO.

For twelve pounds of fruit—seedy preferred—use four pounds of good sugar, making a light syrup, sufficient to cover the fruit, and boil until tender, usually requiring two, or two and a half hours. The fruit looks very nice when pared and cut in round slices, leaving the cores and seeds in.

----:o:----

DELICIOUS APPLES FOR TEA.

MRS. M. G. MOORE.

Take two pounds of apples, pare and core, then slice them into a pan; add one pound of white sugar, the juice of three lemons, and grated rind of one. Let this boil about two hours, and turn into a mold. Serve cold, with custard or cream.

----:o:----

BAKED PEACHES.

MISS MAMIE VAN DOREN.

Peel and place your peaches in a baking tin, sprinkle liberally on each peach brown sugar, little flour, and a lump of butter. Just before placing in the oven add warm water, sufficient to secure a nice gravy, being careful not to disturb the sugar, flour or butter. Bake until soft, and a light brown.

----:o:----

GREEN TOMATO HIGDEN. .

MRS. M. E. J.

·One peck of green tomatoes, sliced thin and sprinkled with salt. Let stand for twenty-four hours, and drain them. Take twelve large onions and slice them thin. Mix well together a quarter of a pound of mustard, one ounce of cloves, one ounce of ground ginger, one ounce of allspice, one ounce of ground pepper, one bottle of ground mustard, one pound of sugar, and two soup ladles of olive oil. Place a layer of each—the sliced tomatoes and the sliced onions, with the spices between—in a large kettle; cover well with vinegar, and boil gently for three hours.

————:o:————

SPICED FIGS.

MRS. JOHN FOY, SAN BERNARDINO.

One quart of the best vinegar, three pounds of sugar, nine pounds of figs, and two tablespoonfuls of mixed spices, cloves, cinnamon, and a little mace; simmer the fruit in the liquor until tender. Either the purple or the best white figs are delicious prepared in this manner.

————:●:————

EUCHRED FRUIT.

MRS. C. H. BRADLEY.

To seven pounds of fruit take three pounds of sugar, one quart of vinegar, all kinds of spices. Heat vinegar, sugar and spices together, and pour over the fruit boiling hot, three days in succession; seal.

————:o:————

PLUM CATSUP.

MRS. JOHN FOY, SAN BERNARDINO.

Boil together for two hours nine pounds of seeded plums, six pounds of sugar, and three pints of the best cider vinegar. Just before removing from the fire add one tablespoonful each of cloves and allspice.

————:o:————.

PRESERVED FIGS.

MRS. S. C. HUBBELL.

Select fine, large, white figs, as near as possible, of equal ripeness, peel and weigh them. Boil slowly until tender, but not broken; take them out with care, and lay on platters. Throw away the liquor and prepare a thick syrup of sugar, as many pounds as of fruit; boil it well, and skim it. Put in the figs and cook slowly till transparent; when nearly done, add a few slices of lemon. Put in glass jars.

PICKLE DEPARTMENT.

TOMATO CATSUP.

MRS. E. F. SPENCE.

Three gallons of tomato juice, three pints of vinegar, nine tablespoonfuls of salt, six tablespoonfuls of black pepper, one tablespoonful of cayenne, five tablespoonfuls of cloves, three tablespoonfuls of allspice, three tablespoonfuls of cinnamon, three tablespoonfuls of mustard. Boil until the usual consistency of catsup.

———:o:———

TOMATO CATSUP.

MRS. J. G. EASTMAN.

To one gallon of strained tomato juice add four tablespoonfuls of mustard, four tablespoonfuls of black pepper, four tablespoonfuls of salt, three tablespoonfuls of cinnamon, two tablespoonfuls of allspice, one tablespoonful of cloves, two tablespoonfuls of cayenne pepper, three pods of green pepper, one teacupful of sugar, one quart of vinegar. Boil three hours, stirring frequently. The vinegar should not be added until the juice and spices are nearly done. When cold, bottle and seal.

———:o:———

PICCALILLI.

MRS. E. S. CHASE.

One gallon of sliced tomatoes (green). Salt them in layers and let them stand all night; drain in the morning; cut six green peppers fine and spread over the top. Take one tablespoonful of black pepper, one ounce of stick-cinnamon, and one ounce of cloves. Boil the whole mixture in sufficient vinegar to cover it, until it is tender—about two hours, moderately. Put up in cans while hot, and cover tightly.

————:o:————
TOMATO CATSUP.

MRS. G. W. WELLS.

To one gallon of pulp put half a pint of vinegar, one teacupful of sugar, one tablespoonful of cinnamon, one tablespoonful of cloves, one tablespoonful of salt, half tablespoonful of black pepper, and half teaspoonful of cayenne pepper. Boil down one-half.

————:o:————
SPICED TOMATOES.

MRS. E. F. SPENCE.

For seven pounds of tomatoes take three and a half pounds of sugar, one pint of strong vinegar, one tablespoonful of whole cloves, and three sticks of cinnamon. Boil thirty-five minutes. Put the sugar and vinegar on to boil; remove the skins from the tomatoes and drop in.

————:o:————
CHILI SAUCE.

MRS. STAFFORD, SANTA ANA.

Ten ripe tomatoes, eight green peppers, six onions, one tablespoonful of salt, one-half cupful of sugar, one quart of vinegar; chop onions, pepper and tomatoes very fine; boil all together two hours.

The above is the finest sauce I ever used, and bottled will keep years.

————:o:————
PRESERVED WALNUTS.

MRS. JOHN MILNER.

Use full-grown nuts, when still green and in milk, before they begin to harden (the best time here to take them from the tree is generally in the month of May); pierce each nut with a thick needle in several places, and lay them in cold water for about eight days, changing the water three times a day; then boil them, well-covered with water, with a pinch of salt, until soft enough to be easily pierced with a needle; put again in cold water for a couple of days, changing the water three times a day. Then boil in sugar, pound for pound, for

a few minutes, and allow to stand and cool; next day pour
off the sugar, boil it down, and pour over the nuts, the same
to be repeated on the third and fourth day.   On the fifth day
boil the walnuts again with the sugar for a few minutes, adding some cloves and stick cinnamon; and then put the nuts
in glasses or jars.   Let the sugar boil down, and when about
the thickness of syrup, pour over the nuts.   Let them be
well covered with the syrup, and, when cool, close the jars
lightly.   If after three or four days the sugar should have
become thin, pour off and boil once more.   Then fill and
close up your jars tightly.

————:o:————

CHILI SAUCE.

MRS. M. G. MOORE.

Forty-eight ripe tomatoes, eight green peppers, eight large
onions, eight teacupfuls of vinegar, eight tablespoonfuls of
salt, eight tablespoonfuls of brown sugar, eight teaspoonfuls
of ginger, eight teaspoonfuls of cinnamon, eight teaspoonfuls of allspice, eight teaspoonfuls of cloves, eight teaspoonfuls of Worcestershire sauce.   Bake four hours.

————:o:————

CHILI SAUCE.

MISS LILLIE E. BASHFORD, OAKLAND.

Nine large tomatoes scalded, two teacupfuls of vinegar,
one onion chopped, three small peppers.   Boil one hour; add
one teaspoonful of cloves, one teaspoonful of allspice, two
teaspoonfuls of sugar, one teaspoonful of ginger, two teaspoonfuls of salt.

————:o:————

MANGOES OF EITHER CANTALOUPE OR CU-
CUMBER.

MRS. ANNA OGIER.

To thirty cantaloupes, when green and about the size
of a large apple—which have been laid in salt brine for a
fortnight and freshened with water till not too salt—it will
take the following ingredients: One pound of horse-radish,
scraped and dried, one pound of ginger, soaked, dried, and
sliced into thin pieces; half pound of white mustard-seed,
the same of black, half pound of cloves, same of black pepper grains, half pound of spice, in grains, one ounce of

mace, two of nutmeg, one of cinnamon, and one of tumeric, half dozen large onions, chopped, two large bunches of celery and an ounce of celery seed, and about two dozen cloves of garlic, which must be skinned, soaked, and dried. Put all these into a large vessel, with about five pounds of brown sugar, and mix with a bottle of good olive oil. Put a gallon of vinegar on to boil, with a little of the stuffing in it, and pour it over the mangoes, which must have a small slice taken out of them. Tie them up carefully with fine twine, to keep the juice on evenly. Let the vinegar cover the mangoes; cover over the top with a thick coat of the oil, and let them stand for three or four months undisturbed. My mother, who was a famous housekeeper, made her mangoes a year in advance, as they are greatly improved by age.

Yellow oil mangoes require the same ingredients, with the addition of a bag of turmeric, which must be put in the jar of vinegar, with a few spices, and set in the sun for several months; and the mangoes must be taken out of the brine, and laid on a table on a cloth in the sun to bleach. This will, perhaps, take four days. You can bleach young corn and beans to put in the stuffing.

————:o:————

SWEET PEAR PICKLES.

MRS. R. M. WIDNEY.

To one pint of good vinegar take four pounds of brown sugar, a quarter of a pound of cinnamon stick, and a quarter of a pound of cloves. Tie up the spices in small bags, and boil with sugar and vinegar till a good syrup is formed. Put in Bartlett or Sickle pears; place on the back of the stove; cover closely, and cook very slowly, until they can be pierced through with a straw.

————:o:————

CHOWDER.

MRS. C. G. DU BOIS.

One peck of green tomatoes chopped fine, sprinkle a good quantity of salt over and let it stand till morning; then squeeze out all the juice. Add one dozen of green peppers, chopped fine, and some horseradish, and cover with weak vinegar, letting it come to a boil; then drain off, and mix with it two tablespoonfuls of cloves, four tablespoonfuls of white mustard-seed, three tablespoonfuls of cinnamon, and one tablespoonful of black pepper. Put into jars and cover with fresh vinegar. Onions chopped fine can be added, if liked.

———:o:———

GRAPE CATSUP.

L. M. THOMPSON.

Five cupfuls of pulp or juice, one cupful of brown sugar, one cupful of vinegar, one teaspoonful of black pepper, one teaspoonful of cloves, one teaspoonful of cinnamon, and one teaspoonful of salt. Boil half away.

———:o:———

FRENCH PICKLES.

MRS. J. HINES.

Take small onions, tomatoes, cauliflowers, and string-beans; cook them in salt and water; when done, bottle, and pour over boiled vinegar, which has been thickened with mustard.

———:o:———

MARTENAS BEANS.

MRS. ANNA OGIER.

Pour boiling salt water over the beans every other day for two weeks; then boil chopped onions and sugar, according to the quantity of beans used—about four pounds to a half peck. Put spices, pepper, cloves, and cinnamon in the vinegar, and pour over while boiling hot; repeat five or six times. A most delicious pickle, but resemble pickled *rats*.

———:o:———

GREEN PEPPER PICKLES.

MRS. M. G. MOORE.

If you prefer your peppers less pungent, cut an opening in the top of each and take out half the seeds. Lay them for two weeks in salt and water, which will bear an egg. Be careful to keep them covered with the brim, by putting some weight on them, and take off the scum as it rises. If they are not yellow at the end of two weeks, let them remain a little longer. When yellow, take them out, wash and put them into a kettle with cold water, cover the tops with grape-vine leaves, and place near the fire; let them get hot, but not

---

simmer. When they are greened in this manner, take them out, drain, place them in your jars, and pour cold, spiced vinegar over them. If you wish to stuff them, chop some cabbage and green cucumbers very fine; season it highly with mace, cinnamon, cloves and mustard-seed. Stuff each pepper with this preparation, and tie a thread around it. I find the Bell pepper here too mild to soak.

PICKLED LIMES.

RELIABLE.

Cut the limes and fill with salt; put them in the sun to dry, and when dry (in two or three weeks), wash off the salt and put them in a jar, in alternate layers with the following spices: allspice, cloves, white mustard-seed, and sliced horse-radish. Fill up the jar with hot vinegar, and let it remain for about four weeks, when they will be ready for use.

CURRANT CATSUP.

MRS. C. H. BRADLEY.

Five pounds of currants, three pounds of sugar, one pint of vinegar, one tablespoonful of allspice, one tablespoonful of cinnamon, one tablespoonful of ground cloves, one-half tablespoonful of salt, and one-half tablespoonful of pepper. Boil two hours over a slow fire.

SWEET–PICKLE PEACHES.

MRS. ANNA OGIER.

To seven pounds of fruit, four pounds of sugar, one quart of vinegar, and one-half pound of cloves and cinnamon. Put the vinegar, sugar, and spices on to boil. Pare the peaches and drop in, letting them boil till soft enough to pierce with a straw. Take them out, put them in a jar, and when the vinegar has boiled an hour longer, pour it over the peaches while hot.

BLACKBERRY PICKLES.

MRS. A. N. HAMILTON.

Twelve pounds of blackberries, three pounds of sugar, one quart of vinegar, three ounces of cloves. Put all together in a porcelain kettle, and scald, but do not boil. Let them stand twenty-four hours; then pour out the vinegar from the berries, and scald; pour back; let stand twenty-four hours; then scald all together and they are done.

——:o: – ——

SPICED BLACKBERRIES.

MRS. F. D. BOVARD.

Take fresh, firm blackberries, and fill glass jars. Make a syrup of seven pounds of sugar, one pint of vinegar, ten cents worth of cinnamon bark, five cents worth of cloves. Boil ten minutes; pour over the berries, and seal.

——:o:——

SWEET-PICKLE DAMSONS.

MRS. ANNA OGIER.

Prick the fruit with a needle, to prevent their bursting; put them in a jar; boil a quart of vinegar to ten pounds of the fruit, four pounds of sugar, and two tablespoonfuls of ground cloves and cinnamon; pour it over the fruit, and let it stand till the third day; boil it again and pour it over the fruit; do this every third day till you have boiled and poured it over the fruit seven times, when it will be ready for use.

CANDY DEPARTMENT.

LEMON CANDY.

MRS. M. M. BOVARD.

Stir briskly in a porcelain-lined saucepan two cupfuls of white sugar, one of water, and three tablespoonfuls of vinegar. Try in water, as for molasses candy; turn into buttered dishes, and work as soon as cool enough to handle. Flavor before pouring into the buttered dishes. The secret of success is not to stir after it begins to boil.

POP-CORN CANDY.

MISS MAMIE VAN DOREN.

Pop, salt, and pound the corn very fine; then take two cupfuls of molasses, one cupful of sugar, one teaspoonful of vinegar, and cook until done; then add one teaspoonful of butter, and stir well a moment or two; then stir in your corn until thick. Remove; do not pull, but when cold cut into square pieces.

BUTTER-SCOTCH.

MISS BERTHA LINDLEY.

Three tablespoonfuls of molasses, two tablespoonfuls of sugar, two tablespoonfuls of water, one tablespoonful of butter. Add a pinch of soda before taking up.

CREAM CANDY.

MRS. GEN. STONEMAN.

To three pounds of white sugar pour water enough to cover, and let the sugar dissolve well. Boil it up once and skim clear, then put in one large tablespoonful of flour, with a little water, and about one-third of a pound of butter.

Just before it is taken from the stove put in a tablespoonful of vanilla. Try it in cold water, to see if it is done. Pour it in well-buttered dishes, or on a marble-slab. Use great care in pulling it, so as not to twist it. Wash your table and sprinkle it with powdered sugar; let the candy lay on it till perfectly stiff; then put it in a glass jar. In moving the boiled sugar be very careful not to jar it, as it would candy it.

————:o:————

TAFFY.

MRS. S. B. CASWELL.

Two cupfuls of brown sugar, two tablespoonfuls of molasses, two tablespoonfuls of butter, and two tablespoonfuls of water.

————:o:————

CHOCOLATE CARAMELS.

RELIABLE.

One cupful each of grated chocolate, milk and molasses, one and one-half cupfuls of sugar, a piece of butter the size of an egg. Melt the butter, then put in the sugar; when this boils, put in the other ingredients, adding, after a while, a tablespoonful of vinegar. Boil till it drops hard.

————:o:————

CORN-BALLS.

MRS. S. B. CASWELL.

One-half cupful of molasses, one-half cupful of sugar, one-half cupful of water, and a piece of butter about the size of a walnut.

————:o:————

CREAM CANDY.

MISS MAMIE VAN DOREN.

Two cupfuls of molasses, one cupful of sugar, half cupful of milk or cream, a lump of butter the size of an egg, a little soda and a little lemon.

————:o:————

SUGAR CANDY.

MISS EMMA BRADLEY.

Stir half cupful of cold water in three cupfuls of white sugar, and boil slowly, stirring constantly. Test by a few drops thrown into a cup of cold water. When nearly done, add a pinch of soda and a teaspoonful of butter.

————:o:————

CHOCOLATE CANDY.

MISS EMMA BRADLEY.

Two large cupfuls of brown sugar, one large teaspoonful of butter, half cupful of water, and a cupful of grated chocolate. Pour thin upon buttered plates, and when nearly cold, score in squares.

COFFEE.

TO BROWN COFFEE.

MRS. C. G. DU BOIS.

Take Java, or one part of Java and one part of a good article of Rio; pick out all the black grains, stones, etc.; wash clean, drain, and put into a pan, placing it in a slow oven until the grains become a dark yellow; then increase the heat, as the grains should brown and swell rapidly, being careful not to let them burn or look as if the oil had come to the surface. Stir frequently. It is done when you can crack the grains by pressing hard between your thumb and finger, and should be of a light brown color. Before taking from the oven stir in a little butter, letting it dry in for a minute or two; then place in a can immediately, covering tight.

————:o:————

COFFEE.

MRS. I. R. DUNKELBERGER.

Equal weights of old Java and Mocha will insure strength and aroma. If a roaster is not available, the coffee should be dried in an oven, with the door open, one or two hours before roasting; then set on the fire in an iron pan and stirred constantly until it becomes a light brown. To ascertain positively when it is done, bite one of the lightest colored kernels; if it is brittle, the whole is done. To make one quart of coffee grind one large cup of coffee, put it into the pot with one egg and sufficient cold water to moisten the whole, and allow it to stand until the coffee swells; then pour on boiling water, and place it over the fire long enough to reach the boiling point; take off; let it stand five minutes; turn it off into another pot, and send it to the table to be served with boiled cream. Coffee is best when roasted, ground and made within one hour. A few minutes before taking from the fire stir in a piece of butter, half the size of an egg. Be sure it is thoroughly incorporated, and it will tend to preserve the strength of coffee, browned to last several days.

———:o:———

CARE OF COFFEE-POT.
MRS. R. M. WIDNEY.

Never allow cold coffee or grounds to remain in your coffee-pot. Empty, wash thoroughly, and dry well, as soon as the meal at which you have used coffee is over. If cold coffee remains it can be used to wet the fresh-ground coffee for the next morning. A fruitful cause of much of the poor coffee is a poorly-kept coffee-pot.

———:o:———

TO MAKE COFFEE.
MRS. C. G. DU BOIS.

Take two heaping tablespoonfuls of ground coffee to each pint of water; stir into this the white of an egg, and dampen with cold water; upon this pour the boiling water, and let it boil fifteen or twenty minutes, keeping it so close that the steam and aroma cannot escape. Take from the stove, pour in a little cold water to settle it, and after standing a moment or so it is ready to serve. An excellent way to get the pure aroma is to reserve one-third of the coffee, adding it about five minutes before removing from the stove.

ADDENDA.
——

REMEDY FOR MOTHS.
MRS. M. G. MOORE.

One ounce of gum-camphor, one ounce of powdered-shell of red pepper; all macerated in eight ounces of strong alcohol for several days, and then strained. With this tincture the furs or clothes are sprinkled and rolled up in sheets. It does not stain.

———:o:———

ORANGE ICE.

MRS. L. CHEEK.

The juice of six oranges and two lemons, mixed with one pint of cold water, in which has been dissolved one quart of sugar. Freeze the same as ice cream.

———:o:———

QUICK PUFFS.

MRS. H. K. W. BENT.

One egg, one cupful of flour, and one cupful of sweet milk. Beat the egg very light; add the flour and milk gradually, to prevent lumping, and pour in very hot gem irons. This should make eighteen or twenty puffs.

———:o:———

TO REMOVE FRUIT, COFFEE OR TEA STAINS.

L. M. THOMPSON.

Hold the spot over a pail, and pour boiling water, from a considerable height, through it. Soap sets the stains, and should never be allowed to touch them.

———:o:———

OX-TAIL SOUP.

MRS. J. E. HOLLENBECK.

One joint of beef, well filled with marrow, and two ox-tails, cut up small. Let it come to a boil; skim it well; let it boil an hour and a half; then cut up half a pound of okra small; put in salt, a little red pepper, and a handful of rice. The vegetables are to be put in whole and removed with the beef when the soup is done. Let the soup boil five or six hours.

———:o:———

BEST HOP YEAST.

MRS. C. G. DU BOIS.

Take five potatoes and one handful of hops, and boil in two quarts of water. After mashing the potatoes, add one tablespoonful of flour, one of molasses, half cupful of brown sugar, and half cupful of salt. Scald all with the two quarts of water. When cool add one teacupful of yeast; leave it in a warm place for twenty-four hours, stirring often. It will not rise, but ferment. The oftener it is stirred the better. Then jug it.

————:o:————

ICE CREAM.

MRS. L. CHEEK.

One quart of good cream, a large coffee cupful of sugar; well-beaten, and flavor to taste.

————:o:————

PRESSED BEEF.

MRS. H. K. W. BENT.

The best piece for this purpose is what is called at the market a "shank." Boil till the meat is ready to fall from the bones, and remove from the kettle to cool. Boil down the broth to about a pint, and add half a box of Cox's gelatine, soaked till soft. Chop the meat—including the fat and soft gelatine—very fine, and season to taste with salt, pepper, made mustard, and herbs. Pour over it the broth, pack closely, and set aside, under a heavy weight, till next day. It will turn out solid, and shave in thin slices.

————:o:————

CAMPHOR ICE.

MRS. L. CHEEK.

Two ounces of almond oil, two ounces of spermaceta, one ounce of camphor gum, one ounce of white wax; melted together.

————:o:————

SUNDAY MORNING MUFFINS.

MRS. H. K. W. BENT.

One tablespoonful of butter, two-thirds of a cupful of sugar, two eggs, one cupful of sweet milk, three cupfuls of flour, and one teaspoonful of baking-powder. Drop in hot gem irons and bake brown in a quick oven.

————:o:————

INVINCIBLES.

RELIABLE.

When the dough for light bread is ready for the oven, take a sufficient quantity and roll it out about one-eighth of an inch thick; cut in squares or lengths of two or three inches; bake in a dry frying-pan on top of the stove, over a hot fire. To be eaten hot, with sweet butter.

www.ingramcontent.com/pod-product-compliance
Lightning Source LLC
Chambersburg PA
CBHW020544270326
41927CB00006B/708